THE
INTRAPRENEUR'S GUIDE
TO PATHFINDING

First published in softback print in the
USA by the League of Intrapreneurs.

ISBN-13 978-0-578-56510-1

Visit our website at www.leagueofintrapreneurs.com

Written by the League of Intrapreneurs
Marjorie Brans, Maggie De Pree, and Florencia Estrade
Illustrated by Tom Jennings (tomjennings.me)
Designed by Charlotte Cline (onemanband.studio)

"We are called upon to do something new, to
confront a no man's land, to push into a forest
where there are no well-worn paths and from
which no one has returned to guide us. To live
in the future means to leap into the unknown,
and this requires a degree of courage for which
there is no immediate precedent and which few
people realize."

ROLLO MAY, THE COURAGE TO CREATE

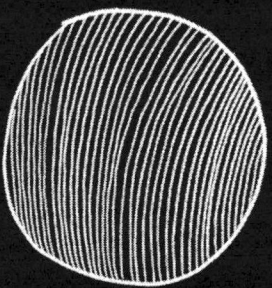

TABLE OF CONTENTS

If you need a quick boost, Energy Bars can be found on pages 12, 22, 40, 46, 50, 66, 76, 82, 94, 138, 142, 148, 163.

When we launched the League of Intrapreneurs in 2012, it was based on a hunch—a sense that within our most traditional institutions, from corporations to governments to charities, there was a healthy and growing impatience with the status quo. Employees from back offices to boardrooms were seeing the limits of "business as usual" to address real and pressing societal challenges—everything from violent conflict to climate change. Instead of lamenting this inadequacy, these people were taking action, stepping up and out to create societal change through their day jobs. We called these people "social intrapreneurs."

Today, the League of Intrapreneurs is a learning community of hundreds of innovators inside big companies like the BMW Group, Merck, and Nestle; inside non-governmental organizations (NGOs) like WWF, CARE, and Friends of the Earth; and inside governments such as the City of Vancouver and the Australian Federal Government. Our members share a belief that we can reprogram our corporations, charities, and regulators with fresh insight and perspective, while bringing deep empathy and humanity to the workplace. Ultimately, we believe we can harness the assets of our most influential institutions to change the world.

Intrapreneurship is gaining momentum as organizations seek to innovate for the challenges of the 21st century. The need for new leadership skills, business models, and systems solutions has been put into sharper focus with the COVID-19 pandemic. While we still have a job to do in raising awareness about the value of intrapreneurship, it is equally important to find and connect intrapreneurs to learn from each other and to develop and share practical tools to drive systems change from within.

This *Pathfinding Guide* is an evolution of our League of Intrapreneurs Toolkit, published in 2013. Like the original, it has been lovingly co-created with our global community of intrapreneurs. We are grateful for the wisdom and generosity of this group of changemakers and would especially like to thank Marjorie Brans for midwifing this *Guide* into existence, Charlotte Cline for her creative design genius, Tom Jennings for bringing the journey to life through illustrations, and Sarah Chee and Jennie Tao for editing and helping take this over the finish line. Also, we extend our thanks to the scores of intrapreneurs and League catalysts for reviewing and inputting into various versions of this *Guide*, notably: Shauna Alexander, Michel Bachmann, Teodora Berkova, Tessa Blencowe, Gib Bulloch, Alexa Clay, Alda Marina Campos, Gwendal Castellan, Maggie De Pree, Sofia Diaz-Rivera, Florencia Estrade, Justin DeKoszmovszky, Tom Farrand, Boris Hesser, Heiko Hosomi Spitzeck, Ian Howatt, Peter Jin Hong, Jeongtae Kim, Antoinette Klatzky, Chryssa Koulis, Rosario Londoño, Tim Mahlberg, Colleen McCormick, Sam McCracken, Milana Momcilovic, Thando Moutlana, Lorena Muiño, Saidah Nash Carter, Caitlin O'Neill-Gutierrez, Ryan Shepard, Katie Sims, Kaushik Sridhar, Angel St. Jean, Miki Stricker-Talbot, Val Thomas, Lucas Urbano, Irene Vance, Daniel Vennard, Brian Watson, and Julian Weber.

And our deepest gratitude to Gifford Pinchot III for coining the term intrapreneurship and continuing to stoke the fire.

This *Pathfinding Guide* has been made possible by the generous support of Comic Relief who are exploring the role of intrapreneurs in shaking up traditional charity models. We are also grateful for the support from the Heron Foundation and the BMW Foundation Herbert Quandt who understand the important role intrapreneurs play in catalyzing systems change.

"The flight itself lasted just one hour 48 minutes. Nevertheless, it was a journey that no one else had ever made, and the cosmonaut faced unknown problems. No one had ever been in space, and it was not at all certain what the experience might reveal. Were human beings suited for space at all? Might something unthinkable occur when he rode in orbit? Might he go mad, or burst, or suffer unusual symptoms? It is reported, however, that Gagarin remained calm throughout. No doubt his composure was one of the reasons he was chosen for the unique honor of being the first man in space. "I see Earth! I see the clouds! It's beautiful, what beauty!" he commented."

**PETER ACKROYD,
ESCAPE FROM EARTH: VOYAGES THROUGH TIME**

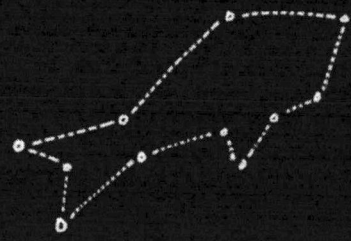

The history of human exploration extends so far back into the archaeological record that anthropologists remain unsure of how Homo sapiens spread around the world. Among the earliest documented pathfinders were the Polynesian people, seafarers unmatched in their skill of roaming blue-water seas, who started exploring as early as 5,000 years before the modern era.

Settling on islands north of New Guinea, they had traveled over 2,000 miles to reach Tonga by 2,846. By 1,000 AD, navigators Kupe, Mo'ikeha, and Hotu Matu'a had discovered New Zealand, Hawai'i, and the world's most remote inhabited island, Rapa Nui (a.k.a. Easter Island), off the coast of Chile. They accomplished these feats of oceanic exploration in artisanal canoes long before European explorers Vasco de Gama and Christopher Columbus set forth by ship in search of riches and conquest.

The Polynesians discovered new land with no tools for navigation other than their intimate knowledge of the oceans, the waves and swell formations, the underside patterns of clouds, the stars, and the flight patterns of land-based birds.[1]

In the modern era, our endlessly adventurous species has now explored nearly every corner of land on Earth. And our way of life and impact on earth has been so significant in the past few centuries that scientists have declared a new, distinct geological age: the Anthropocene.[2] This is an epoch of human activity that has set a new trajectory for all living systems on Earth. Over 1,300 cities have declared climate emergencies,[3] 1 million plant and animal species are threatened with extinction,[4] and resources are unequally distributed with the richest 1 percent owning 45 percent of the world's wealth.[5]

We celebrate the human ingenuity that has increased expectations and expanded boundaries in areas such as quality of life, health, technology, work, and wealth. But our economic system is reaching its expiration date.

Our communities— global and local—are facing systems challenges on a scale never seen before, from pandemics to poverty, climate change to violent conflict.

This moment requires us to rediscover our ancient pathfinding instincts—not to search for new land, but to discover new economic and societal models that will enable us to thrive in harmony with one another and with our environment. Why pathfinding? Because there is no roadmap to a just, healthy, and sustainable future. As the COVID-19 global pandemic has demonstrated, we must increasingly master the art of navigating in uncertainty and adapting and responding to challenges, shocks and opportunities in real time all while keeping our eye on our "North Star."

The good news (yes, there is good news) is that there is a large and growing movement of people navigating this new terrain—whether you call it sustainable development, sustainability, social innovation, or Doughnut Economics. Social entrepreneurs and citizen activists are at the forefront of this movement, giving birth to new sustainable models that are making old ones obsolete.

Less visible are the change agents working to transform our system from the inside. People who are bringing new, more equitable ways of doing business, introducing different thinking, and challenging the status quo. Social intrapreneurs are the modern workplace's explorers. We believe they will help lead the world's incumbent institutions into 21st century sustainability. But getting there will require setting forth bravely into the unknown, battling the professional equivalent of storms and river crossings, blazing new trails in domains of practice, hacking paths through tangled bureaucracy, and pushing through the muck of political swamps. It will require resilience, ingenuity, bravery, and a love of adventure.

Unlike survival books that help readers get out of hairy situations, this book is about moving into them. Pathfinding is the practice of managing by your wits, finding comfort in discomfort, and moving ahead, all the while being unsure of what awaits at the end of the journey. We've written this *Guide* for aspiring and practicing intrapreneurs alike. If you are an intrapreneur, you likely share our belief that when you engage in a career based on values, personal authenticity, and courage in the face of uncertainty, you experience a deep sense of fulfillment, meaning, and beauty in work and life.

We hope this *Pathfinding Guide* will help you and your co-travelers venture wisely and joyfully.

How to Use This Guide

Reading this manual, you'll begin to develop your own approach to modern-day pathfinding, applying ancestral practices and philosophies in ways that feel contemporary and fresh.

Being prepared and knowing what to do when a challenging intrapreneurial situation arises requires training and practice, which is what makes this *Guide* a valuable element in your career training plan. Read it cover to cover, by chapter, or in sections. Learn the information and practice the skills. Don't wait until you're in professional quicksand to familiarize yourself with the techniques, philosophy, and case studies.

In the pages ahead, we'll explore how to chart a destination; move with your teammates through uneven terrain in low visibility conditions; stay the course using a project compass; navigate the system and tap into energy sources for an intrapreneurial project; sustain your efforts when you encounter setbacks in the wild; and use your self-esteem as a flotation device.

Sprinkled throughout this *Guide* are what we call "Energy Bars"—success and survival stories from League members and other intrapreneurs. These accounts give you a perspective on intrapreneurship in the real world, at different levels of complexity and experience levels. Note that for the sake of brevity, going forward in this *Guide* when we use the term intrapreneurship, we mean social intrapreneurship that seeks to contribute to a better world for people and planet.

As you work your way through the book, you may see an intrapreneurial plan emerge. This book's companion, *The Intrapreneur's Compass*, offers you exercises and tools to practice your new pathfinding knowledge and skills.

You can find it at leagueofintrapreneurs.com.

Defining Social Intrapreneurship Across Sectors

Forbes Magazine identifies entrepreneurs as people who "identify a need—any need—and fill it."[6] Purpose-driven social entrepreneurs typically fill social and environmental needs by starting new socially-minded businesses or organizations or movements. Social intrapreneurs are close cousins to social entrepreneurs, but they operate nearer to the center of formal authority and power by working in well-established organizations.

Social Intrapreneurship, n. "An autonomous process through which individuals or groups of individuals seek to identify and exploit entrepreneurial opportunities that address societal challenges from within established organizations."[7]

We have prepared this guide for intrapreneurs across three sectors: corporate, government, and NGO/ non-profit. Broadly speaking, the challenges of intrapreneurs in any big institution remain similar across the sectors; however, there are some key differences:

CORPORATE INTRAPRENEURS
Historically, companies— particularly large multinationals— have made it their mission to make money and respond to shareholders. To succeed in the corporate context, intrapreneurs must marry profit with purpose at a large scale.

Examples:
Miriam Turner, founded Net-Works, an inclusive business incubated at global carpet manufacturer, Interface. Net-Works empowers coastal communities in the Philippines and Cameroon to collect and sell used fishing nets which are recycled into yarn for carpet tiles.

Claudia Lorenzo, Vice President, The Coca-Cola Company, created a social initiative called Coletivo to tackle inequality and joblessness among thousands of Brazilian youth.

GOVERNMENT INTRAPRENEURS

Government intrapreneurs operate in a highly political work environment with near constant election-cycle pressures and a culture of risk avoidance. To bring about meaningful change in the public sector, intrapreneurs must earn the trust of elected political officials, and navigate hierarchical structures and tight time frames, all while ensuring that short-term constituent needs are met.

Examples:
Angel St. Jean, Assistant Director for Strategic Initiatives at the City of Baltimore, is leading the effort to build an effective workforce system that removes structural barriers to economic opportunity for residents and at the same time addresses the workforce needs of employers drawn to and growing within a former economic powerhouse town that is currently undergoing a rebirth.

Wilfred Mushagalusa, IT Specialist and Rapid Results Coach, Government of Democratic Republic of Congo, is passionate about engaging citizens in developing effective public services and is training his peers on new methods for innovation and radical collaboration.

NGO/NON-PROFIT INTRAPRENEURS

By definition, NGOs and non-profits operate for the public good. One of the biggest challenges for intrapreneurs in this sector is severely limited resources. Management is often so focused on keeping the lights on that workers frequently find themselves pursuing the next grant at the expense of chasing outcomes. Often the most successful NGO/non-profit intrapreneurs are those who can show how their innovations generate income as well as impact.

Examples:
Ryan Shepard, CARE, created a collaborative innovation center to bring new and unlikely participants into developing solutions while leveraging the brand, scale, and resources of CARE.

Eddie Jjemba, Red Cross Red Crescent Climate Centre, is fostering climate resilience with urban communities across Africa using participatory methods for learning and dialogue about complex systems.

QUESTIONS TO ASK YOURSELF
Where does my fire come from?
What are my core values?
What is my purpose at work?
Do I have the will and skill to
survive as an intrapreneur?

1

Pathfinding Mindset

The sixth century text *Dao De Jing* gave birth to a saying that has been printed on countless mugs and graduation cards: "A journey of a thousand miles begins with a single step." This wise saying encourages us to stick one brave foot in front of another, but it doesn't say anything about the explorers who willingly step away from the prescribed world of professional ladders and climb toward a career that is defined by more than progressively bigger titles or salary increases.

Before becoming an intrapreneur and pathfinder, it's important to explore your heart first. What are all the reasons you're considering intrapreneurship as a way of showing up at work? Yale School of Management's Amy Wrzesniewski has identified that in every industry and level of hierarchy she has studied, there are always three types of people:

— Workers who have a job

— Workers who are building a career

— Workers who have a calling[8]

Employees with a job often pursue passions outside the office, but while at work, they may do the minimum in order to keep the paycheck coming. Meanwhile, career-oriented professionals may pride themselves on a job well done, while also working toward the next promotion. People with a calling, however, show up to their work differently. Led by their hearts, they connect to the highest possible mission of their organizations.

Wrzesniewski finds that everyone—from CEOs to janitors—falls into one of these three categories. Interviewing the custodial staff at the local hospital in New Haven, she met "job janitors" who see their job as pushing around mops and brooms to earn a living and not as a way to seek purpose. "Career janitors" see their job as simply the first step on the professional ladder. Meanwhile, the "calling janitors" see their jobs as contributing to positive outcomes for patients. For example, they may help people in difficult medical situations recover more quickly by creating clean and cheerful environments. Without being asked, one such calling janitor regularly moved the artwork around in the coma ward, in the hope that doing so might stimulate patients' brains.

– What kind of worker are you?

– What is your purpose?

– What gives your life and work meaning?[9]

If you're in a situation where your only priority or goal is to secure the next paycheck, social intrapreneurship is probably not the right way to go. There are easier ways to make money. Career-focused individuals who like to plan their ascent up the professional ladder may find intrapreneurship an exciting path toward greater recognition, especially in environments where intrapreneurship is rewarded. However, in less intrapreneur-friendly environments, career workers are likely to find the path harder than they expect and to abandon projects quickly when they experience organizational resistance, especially from people senior to them. Indeed, our experience is that calling-driven (purpose-driven) intrapreneurs are the ones most likely to sustain themselves through the long and tough road of a social innovation project. The third type of worker measures success in radically different ways from the other two, and that difference in focus leads to big differences in behavior at every level of the professional hierarchy.

If you're clear about your own purpose, you can work systematically to remove the activities and aspects of your life that drain you of energy. You may ask for a reassignment to a new supervisor or team, or you may feel perhaps that staying put is better. Wherever you are, ask yourself how you can find ways to make a dysfunctional team or organization better for everyone in and affected by it. Spend time remembering or researching what the organization says it's all about. If you see a disconnect between your work unit's purported mission and values, how can you contribute to a better alignment between the organization and its aspirational higher self?

Like the calling janitors, successful social intrapreneurs employ a career strategy known as "job crafting." Job crafting involves actively modifying one's job duties to bring about more engagement and meaning. For some people, crafting may involve subtle shifts in tasks and approaches or taking on small projects to extend their remit. For other employees, it may involve sitting down with a line manager to expand or redesign their job description to allow for more purposeful pursuits.[10]

Note that Wrzesniewski's research supports what we at the League have seen over and over: making intrapreneurial change doesn't require a big title; it requires the right attitude. More often than not, intrapreneurial projects are successfully led by people from the middle to lower layers of the institutional hierarchy (see the story of Sam McCracken on page 12 for a good example of change originating outside the managerial ranks).

Seeing your workplace as an opportunity to serve humanity can change the office from a place of drudgery to a landscape of adventure. You can reframe challenges like arbitrary policies, short-sighted decisions, and misguided priorities into adventure-laden obstacles to overcome. Going into an intrapreneurial project knowing that wild animals are part of the "adventure" will help you avoid experiencing some of the negative aspects of workplaces as soul-depleting. Your mission is to advance life on Earth, reduce the toxicity of the work environment for your colleagues, and help the organization's various stakeholders succeed and thrive—you just need to figure out how to run from one side of a swift river to the other while running over crocodile backs.

JOB JANITORS
Paying the bills

CAREER JANITORS
First step on the ladder

CALLING JANITORS
Contributing to well-being

SAM MCCRACKEN ON MAKING CHANGE FROM WHERE YOU ARE

Sam is a basketball coach and a Native American of the Sioux tribe in the US state of Montana. He also works for Nike, one of the most iconic brands in the world. Sam's community, like many Native American communities, is battling high rates of diabetes. And for Sam, this is personal. His own mother died of complications from type 2 diabetes in 2001.

When Sam embarked on his intrapreneurial journey, he wasn't working in a high-powered executive office. He was working in a warehouse in Wilsonville, Oregon, when he had an idea.

He said to himself, "I work for the biggest sports company in the world. I must be able to do something in my role at Nike to help my community."

He didn't have a grand plan; he simply sensed a need in his community and believed he could help. Sam started working with leaders in his tribe to promote healthy lifestyles by organizing events, such as fun runs and walks. He arranged to provide free or discounted Nike products to incentivize people to take part.

As he saw the momentum around his project grow, he began to share his story with others at the company. Sam's energy was infectious and a team of Nike designers offered to help create products in line with Sam's vision. The result was Nike N7, a line of products that embodied the sustainability values of Native American communities and encouraged kids to get active.

The initiative ultimately developed into the N7 Fund. Since its inception in 2009, the Fund has awarded $5.6 million in grants to 243 communities and organizations, reaching more than 420,000 youth. Harnessing the power of sport as a unifying force, the N7 Fund helps kids reach life goals and reflects Nike's belief in creating more equal playing fields for everyone.

What Are Your Values and Motivations?

Otto Scharmer, Professor at MIT and co-founder of the Presencing Institute, often says that the quality of an innovation or intervention is a function of the attention and intention of the leaders involved. So, understanding your values and motivations will also help you to understand how you may show up at work and help you identify gaps, biases, or potential blind spots.[11]

Your purpose at work will be a function of the values you bring into the world. For instance, if you find yourself striving for perfection at work, you might value professionalism, thoroughness, or pats on the back for a job well done. If you enjoy finding new ways to address old problems, you may value curiosity, creativity, or challenge.

Values are our motivators—the sparks or fires inside us that drive our behavior, conscious or unconscious. If your behaviors and activities at work are out of alignment with your personal values, you may feel a lack of authenticity in your life and in extreme cases, you may experience the psychological crisis of cognitive dissonance.

The deeply-held values and motivations of intrapreneurs help them to stay the course through even the heaviest of headwinds. The "Barrett Seven Levels Model" of consciousness can help intrapreneurs assess their values and motivations. Inspired by Abraham Maslow's "Hierarchy of Needs," Barrett's model describes seven levels of human motivations that apply not only to individuals but also to corporations, governments, and NGOs. At the lowest levels, motivations center around basic survival and stability. At the highest levels, motivations pursue benefits to humanity and the planet.[12]

Using Barrett's model, you can set goals for your personal development as a leader, and also for your intrapreneurial project as a vehicle for growth in organizational consciousness.

As you incorporate new levels of consciousness and your organization does as well, you are likely to experience more productive and satisfying relationships with your workmates and a deeper alignment between your personal purpose and how you show up in the office.

– What are your values?

– Can you clearly articulate them?

– Are you living your values at work?

It's important to note that the personal growth that comes with each new level of consciousness rarely comes without emotional pain. Acknowledging our faults and weaknesses is never easy, and it's sometimes hard to commit to work on them. But when we do, the pain is different than if we avoid the issue. Just as when we go to the gym and lift heavy weights, we may find that our muscles ache and our joints are sore, but this is what psychologists call "clean pain." Clean pain comes with great effort, but also with a sense of relief that we don't have to pretend not to have faults anymore. "Dirty pain," in contrast, comes from denying hard truths and continuing to engage in behavior that may have served us well at one time, but is now maladaptive. After identifying whether you're experiencing clean or dirty pain, you will know if you're on the right track.[13]

When Your Values Align with Your Work

Boris Hesser, an intrapreneur at Merck, a global science and technology company, describes his journey to aligning values at work this way. "I was on a straight corporate development path: a scientist by training with a long career in drug development, then in strategy and portfolio management. However, I always had an interest in population issues and loved the topic of healthcare as it's something really meaningful and is what the world needs." Boris was offered an opportunity to explore a sustainable business model for access to healthcare in Africa.

> "There was a strong match between my values and interests," he explains, "so I took the chance. Social intrapreneurship starts with that: you have to have the guts to take actions towards an inspiring goal that may change the world. Not the whole world, but the world that you can change. This is where it started for me."

The journey is paying off. Boris has launched a pilot project in Kenya, setting up five basic healthcare centers that leverage an existing network of pharmacies serving low-income, remote communities. Each center is staffed with a nurse and pharmacist and internet access to make telehealth consultations with doctors at a distance.

"I suggest to everyone: look in the mirror. Ask yourself: who are you? What are your talents? Use them and do what you love."

SYLVIA A. EARLE, AQUANAUT, OCEANOGRAPHER, SCIENTIST, & RECORD-HOLDER FOR DEEPEST UNTETHERED OCEAN DIVE

Developing the Will and Skill to Survive: Your League IQ

By definition, intrapreneurship involves doing things that the current workplace is not set up to do. As such, any intrapreneurial idea will encounter resistance, and sometimes invite outright attack. You'll need the will and skill to survive these challenges.

Will to Survive

If you have a deep sense of purpose, confidence, mental and physical toughness, and solidarity with other people, you will have the will to survive. It is the will to survive that explains why some aspiring intrapreneurs with little professional experience enjoy significant success, while those with all the professional training, titles, and budget, fail.

Attaining an intimate knowledge of yourself, your motivations, beliefs, and behaviors may come with fear and awkwardness, but the more you grow comfortable with pathfinding in your own soul, the more you'll embrace the challenge and see the benefits for yourself and everyone else who comes into contact with you.

With a strong will to survive, even when you find yourself on the edge of losing your job for having taken a big risk, you may feel that you've never been so alive.

How to Cultivate Your Will to Survive

ARTICULATE YOUR PURPOSE

Know why you want to be an intrapreneur and commit to overcoming obstacles in service to your purpose.

NURTURE A STRONG BODY & MIND

If you don't have one already, adopt a regimen of mental and physical wellness before you embark on the intrapreneurial journey. Guard your mental health. Sleep adequately, eat healthy food, and relax when you are tired.

ACKNOWLEDGE YOUR FEARS

It is natural to worry about rocking the boat and perhaps drawing the disapproval of your colleagues for choosing to show up with all your values at the office. Step back and observe your fears at a distance. Acknowledge that courage isn't about not having fears; it's about having them and choosing to move forward anyway.

THINK POSITIVELY

Seek out inspiring stories of change and share them to promote positive thoughts in others.

CHOOSE HUMOR

A good daily laugh will sustain you through the harder times. Make it a practice to experience joy and spend time with cherished colleagues, family, and friends.

PROMOTE SOLIDARITY & AUTHENTICITY

Model for others what you hope to see become more commonplace at your office. Support others who are stretching in the same direction.

COUNT YOUR SUCCESSES

You will face many setbacks. Intrapreneurship is a challenging professional endeavor, and you should go into it knowing that you'll encounter resistance. Every victory no matter how small is one to celebrate.

Skill to Survive

Will without skill will only get you so far. The skill to survive gives you the extra edge that can be developed and honed over time. In our years of working with intrapreneurs, we have identified six leadership competencies required for effective intrapreneurship.

How to Cultivate Your Skill to Survive

GENERATIVE THINKING

Intrapreneurs are independent and generative thinkers, able to reconcile seemingly opposable tensions by finding new and creative solutions and opportunities. They are great pattern spotters and rely more on trial and error than on logic and reasoning. Confident in their views of what's possible, intrapreneurs enjoy challenging the status quo.

ENTREPRENEURIAL DRIVE

Intrapreneurs are entrepreneurs on the inside. They prefer flexibility and autonomy to being told what to do. Motivated by learning and so-called "wicked challenges," they prefer to be rewarded not just for outcomes, but also for their approaches to solving problems. Work is more than just work; it is about improving the world.

MARKET SHAPING

Intrapreneurs enjoy the special ability to create markets. They do this by focusing deeply on user needs. They also have broader definitions of what is salient to an organization and can translate seemingly unconnected trends, issues, risks, and opportunities into the core priorities of their employers. Intrapreneurs maintain diverse networks and bring together unlikely allies, with a capacity to move from ideas to tangible structures and business models.

NAVIGATING SYSTEMS

Intrapreneurs are experts at navigating the politics of their organizations. They can simultaneously speak to their authentic passions while speaking to an audience of their colleagues. Engaging senior-level support and bringing together stakeholders across organizational silos, they build empathy and social capital.

BUILDING COMMUNITY

Intrapreneurs are natural bridge-builders between external communities and their organizations. They are good listeners and build trust and connections on a human level. At their most mature, they operate with low ego to allow others to share and shape solutions.

UNLOCKING RESOURCES

Intrapreneurs apply creativity and resourcefulness to make things happen. They are flexible and adaptable and know how to do more with less. They are comfortable (and even embrace) uncertainty and approach work with a high-risk appetite. As we heard from one intrapreneur, "the greater risk is in not acting."

Don't worry if you haven't mastered the complete intrapreneurial skill set yet. Even the most seasoned intrapreneurs are constantly learning how to build their capacity for change. These competencies may not reside in just one individual, but may be assembled across an intrapreneurial team. If you feel you are not as strong in one area like "unlocking resources," can you bring someone on board with those skills? Or if you are struggling to navigate the system and office politics, can you engage a senior mentor to help you?

You can gauge your intrapreneurial skill level by taking The League Intrapreneur Quotient™, a quick self-assessment that will measure your strengths and unique gifts and identify areas for learning and development. Developed with Corporate Entrepreneurs LLC's Susan Foley, a seasoned expert in the field, this tool is based on years of research looking at the competencies of successful intrapreneurs and intrapreneurial leaders. A major insight from Susan's research is that intrapreneurs think, work, and act differently from most employees and managers. These differences can be a strength, but self-awareness and your ability to build bridges will be key to your success.

ANONYMOUS INTRAPRENEUR ON
THE WILL AND SKILL TO SURVIVE

One League member, who asked to remain anonymous, shared her experience working for a large NGO as the leader of a staff union. The organization had a sterling global reputation for its human rights work, but there was a troubling truth behind the brand. Internally, many felt the organization wasn't living its values when it came to the treatment of employees.

The situation had deteriorated so much that staff banded together to challenge management through the staff union. In response, the Director of Human Resources (HR) hired a crackerjack law firm to bust the union. What the Director of HR didn't know was that the law firm was infamous for confrontational tactics—in particular for its aggressive treatment of a widely celebrated and legendary union leader. In a twist of irony, this very union leader had been presented a human rights award by the NGO a few years earlier.

The intrapreneurial union team received an anonymous tip that the organization's HR staff was attending conferences on union-busting tactics. The team also felt they were seeing signs that the NGO was making arrangements to push union leaders out of the organization, and it was unclear if they would make it out with their professional reputations "alive." The questionable practices HR staff were learning had been employed by many of the companies the NGO criticized publicly.

The union team had a choice: question the NGO's practices in the media or take their issues to management and demand change. The team had the will to survive and wanted to keep doing the good work the NGO was known for.

Realizing that the brand was valuable to everyone—staff and management—and that the organization's name was the foundation for its programs and fundraising, the team chose to take the embarrassing information to the CEO.

Shocked to learn what was happening, the CEO fired the Director of HR and undertook an investigation. Major changes in management-staff relations followed. Only one year after this incident, everyone, from staff to management, agreed that the organization's internal culture had improved greatly and was in line with the NGO's mission and values.

Between this team's will to survive the attack and the skill to use embarrassing information strategically, these intrapreneurs made a positive change.

QUESTIONS TO ASK YOURSELF
What system am I trying to change?
What are the highest points of impact in this system?
How can I frame my quest as a question?

2

Identifying Your Quest

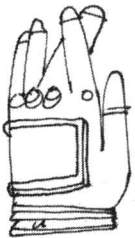

Generative thinking is one of the greatest gifts that intrapreneurs bring to problem solving. They see problems in a wider context or "system" and identify patterns and interconnections that can help unlock solutions where progress has stalled.

For example, Daniel Vennard is an intrapreneur behind the Better Buying Lab at the World Resources Institute. A botanist by training, Daniel worked to advance sustainability for nearly a decade at the global food company, Mars, Inc. During this time, he discovered that nearly a quarter of all planet-warming greenhouse gas emissions come from food production and associated land-use change. Daniel set up the Better Buying Lab, a collaboration of global food corporations, to develop effective branding and marketing strategies to shift consumer behavior toward reduced meat consumption.

At the League, we often use a wave diagram, as illustrated on the next page, to visualize systems change like the one Daniel is trying to bring about.

Catching the "next wave" requires intrapreneurs to employ generative or systems thinking. We see this wave dynamic in action if we think about the mainstreaming of the green movement. The institutions that make the leap before the decline are thriving. Those hanging on to the previous wave without leaping will ride it to decline.

The Generative Leap

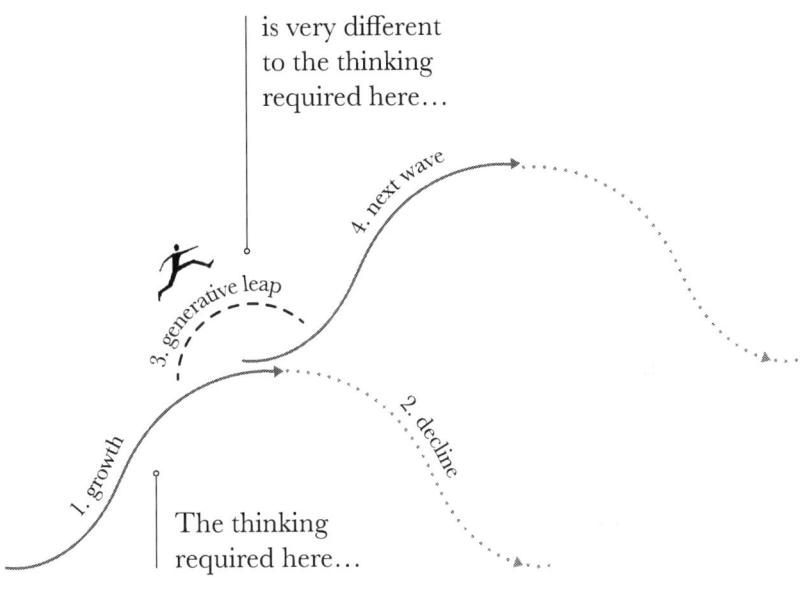

is very different
to the thinking
required here…

The thinking
required here…

Fig. 1. Created by James Parr (founder of the Frontier Development Lab) on the back of a napkin at London coffeehouse in 2007 and adapted by the League of Intrapreneurs.

1. Growth stage of an organization or idea.

2. Decline stage of an organization or idea if it doesn't adapt and change. It will have a natural shelf life.

3. A generative leap is an adaptation to the changing system. If you can time this jump before decline, you are at the highest point to ride the next wave. Intrapreneurs are great at generative leaps.

4. The next wave is the new way of being that will carry you forward to success.

So, What Does it Mean to Think in Systems?

Systems thinking may be more intuitive for some than others, but we can all build this mental capacity. The literature on systems change is often very technical, making it inaccessible to even the most seasoned of intrapreneurs. In our brief introduction to the topic, we focus on the foundational principles. If you want to go deeper, we suggest that you explore the works of Donella H. Meadows, David Stroh, Leyla Acaroglu, Anna Birney, the Santa Fe Institute, and the Berkana Institute.

As defined by Meadows in her book *Thinking in Systems: A Primer*, a system is "a set of things—people, cells, molecules, or whatever—interconnected in such a way that they produce their own pattern of behaviour over time."[14] Systems thinking involves three elements:

1. Seeing the Whole Instead of the Parts

Systems educator and author Draper Kauffman points out that dividing a dairy cow in half doesn't give you two cows. A split cow would no longer be able to function as a "milk producing system."[15] Thinking in systems is about seeing beyond the individual parts toward the whole. The behavior of the system depends on its entire structure and not just on adding up the behavior of its individual parts.

2. Understanding Relationships & Interconnections

A tree doesn't thrive in isolation. It depends on the sun, soil, and water. It may provide shelter to wildlife and provide fruit to people and animals. It also can offer a place to climb, shade for our homes, oxygen to breathe, and beautiful views. The tree is not a single object in isolation, but consists of a series of relationships. Similarly, your organization functions as part of a web of relationships that affect employees, clients, vendors, the general public, natural resources, waste streams, and more.

3. Identifying Root Causes

Often, what first appears to be the problem, isn't. It's only when we take the time to dig deeper, that we uncover the "root cause" of a problem. By identifying the origin of an issue, we can find the places where a small investment can make a big impact. By addressing the root causes of a negative system behavior, we can do something to stop and even reverse this behavior. We discuss this complex task in the next section.

One method we have found helpful for understanding and influencing systems is Theory U, developed by Otto Scharmer with his team at the Presencing Institute. Theory U is a method for innovation. The "U" part of the name refers to the mental shape of the participant journey (see Fig. 2).

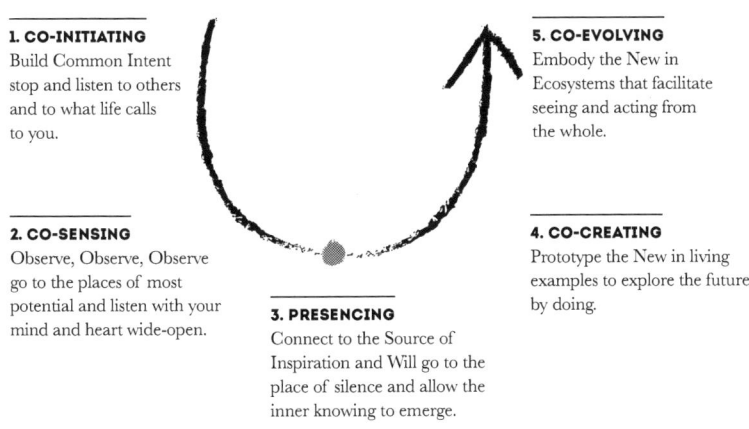

1. CO-INITIATING
Build Common Intent
stop and listen to others
and to what life calls
to you.

5. CO-EVOLVING
Embody the New in
Ecosystems that facilitate
seeing and acting from
the whole.

2. CO-SENSING
Observe, Observe, Observe
go to the places of most
potential and listen with your
mind and heart wide-open.

3. PRESENCING
Connect to the Source of
Inspiration and Will go to the
place of silence and allow the
inner knowing to emerge.

4. CO-CREATING
Prototype the New in living
examples to explore the future
by doing.

Fig. 2. The Theory U illustrates five movements that comprise a journey from one side of the U, down, and up to the other side of the U. Created by the Presencing Institute. From the Presencing Institute website: https://www.presencing.org/aboutus/theory-u.

Theory U is a collective process that requires identifying and enlisting diverse stakeholders across the system you wish to change. Together, you will create a common intention to pursue over a period of time (six months, one year, two years, or more). As we know, systems change is a long process, but you can also advance in sprints. A shared intention could be getting more people to take public transport, encouraging less meat consumption, or creating more opportunities for youth employment.

Once you have aligned around your intention—the system you want to shift and outcomes you are seeking, you then move through the next four phases of Theory U.

Co-sensing. Together your team immerses itself in the system which you are trying to shift. Methods include interviews, site visits, and other types of experiential learning. The key in this stage is to listen and observe deeply without judgment. Open space for new perspectives and let go of assumptions that may not serve you or may be standing in the way of impactful solutions.

Presencing. The idea behind presencing is that when we start letting go of our strongly held beliefs and assumptions and lower our egos, new, powerful perspectives and ideas can emerge. Presencing is about uncovering blind spots and opportunities by creating a safe space to look at an issue with new eyes and greater understanding. The Presencing Institute has developed several methods such as 3-D and 4-D modeling to help groups uncover these new possibilities.

Co-creating. Once you have identified your opportunities, the fun really begins. You can start co-creating potential solutions. This iterative innovation process has been well developed by groups like IDEO. But, having done the hard work of sensing the system and presencing, you will be asking better questions to frame your innovation. This is the time for prototypes.

Co-evolving. The final stage of the journey is about moving beyond individual solutions to shifting the entire system. Once you have tested a few prototypes, the next step is to review what has been learned and which prototypes might have the highest impact. It is important to involve external stakeholders and sectors in this assessment. This is the time to connect high-leverage prototypes with the institutions and players that can help take it to the next level of piloting and scaling.

What we particularly like about the Theory U framework is the principles upon which it is based. First, the approach focuses on radical collaboration, acknowledging that no one individual or organization can address a systems challenge on its own. Theory U refers to radical collaboration as moving from an "ego-system" to an "ecosystem": shifting our awareness from our own needs to include the needs of a wider group of actors. Second, it acknowledges that the quality of any social intervention reflects the quality of the intervenors, specifically the intervenors' awareness or consciousness.

Have you ever experienced a sense of flow in your work or perhaps through your hobbies? Maybe you've participated in a sports team where you were so in sync with your teammates that communication was happening almost as a "sixth sense," where you were effortlessly moving and working together to win your game. The team at the Presencing Institute says that flow and deeper levels of consciousness like this are critical for innovators working together to shift systems.

Intrapreneur Antoinette Klasky and her team at the Eileen Fisher Institute have been integrating Theory U methods into their regular work practice. Antoinette says, "Theory U is about letting go of old patterns of thought and action and operating from a place of curiosity, compassion, and courage ... It's an invitation to go beyond limited singular worldviews to a space of what's needed on a collective level."[16]

"We can't solve problems by using the same kind of thinking we used when we created them."

ALBERT EINSTEIN

Shifting the Conditions That Hold the Problem in Place

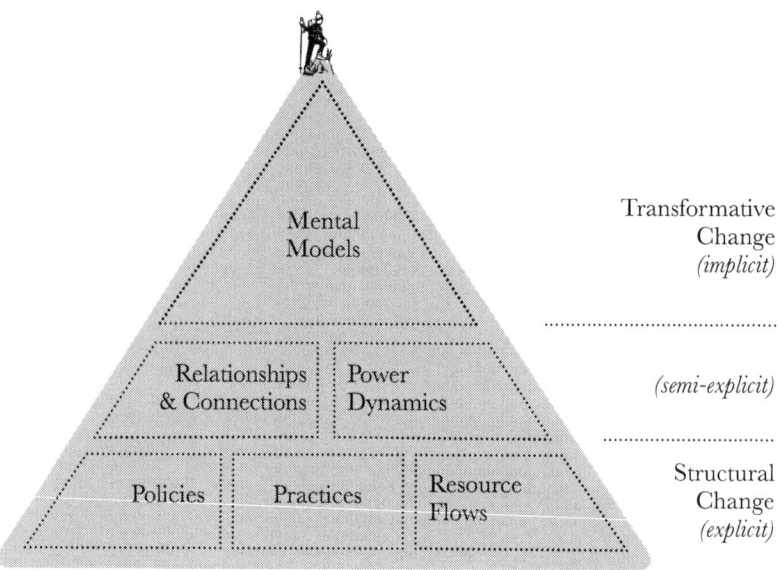

Fig. 3. Adapted from FSG's The Water of Systems Change.
From FSG. https://www.fsg.org/publications/water_of_systems_change.

Tackling Root Causes

In "The Water of Systems Change," the social consulting firm FSG lists six conditions that hold complex system problems in place:

1. Policies

Government, institutional, and organizational rules, regulations, and priorities that guide the actions of any entity.

2. Practices

Espoused activities of institutions, coalitions, networks, and other entities targeted to improving social and environmental progress. Also, within the entity, the procedures, guidelines, or informal shared habits that comprise work.

3. Resource Flows

How money, people, knowledge, information, and other assets such as infrastructure are allocated and distributed.

4. Relationships & Connections

The quality of connections and communication occurring among actors in the system, especially among those with differing histories and viewpoints.

5. Power Dynamics

The distribution of decision-making power, authority, and both formal and informal influence among individuals and organizations.

6. Mental Models

Habits of thought—deeply-held beliefs and assumptions and taken-for-granted ways of operating that influence how people think, what they do, and how they talk.[17]

So, how can we use FSG's hierarchy of systems conditions to create impact at key leverage points in a given system? Let's use an example. Taci Abreu is Head of Marketing at the Brazilian lifestyle and clothing brand FARM Rio and is working to reduce waste in her industry. Here's how she might hypothetically go about doing that at a systems level. Note that she may tackle any one of the six conditions in any order.

Practices:

Taci's jumping-off point is to influence the design practices of her colleagues to maximize the use of their raw materials and to start replacing virgin materials with recycled materials.

Resource Flows:

Taci next considers how to unlock investment in new textile technologies, like long-lasting or self-cleaning materials that extend the life of the clothes her company produces.

Relationships & Connections:

But, still tons of clothes are ending up in landfill. So, she begins exploring partnerships with organizations in her system, like libraries, grocery stores, and other retailers to create a "take-back scheme" for used clothing. This initiative ensures that clothes get recycled instead of getting dumped.

Power Dynamics:

Taci hears about a trend called open source innovation: engaging customers and citizens to help solve so-called wicked challenges. So, she decides to run a hackathon to enable customers and design students to come up with disruptive ideas for reducing waste in the industry.

Mental Models:

One of the hackathon's winning ideas is to rent clothes rather than sell them, thereby shifting consumers' mental model of clothing as something one owns to clothing as a service. Taci sets up a prototype shop for renting clothing and joins forces with other leading brands and NGOs to catalyze a #dontbuythis #rentthis movement.

Policies:

A local politician catches wind of the movement and pursues legislation for a mandatory take-back scheme for fashion retailers.

As this example shows, systems interventions often come about when intrapreneurs start with one solution and then realize that there is a higher point of leverage in the system. It's not always clear what those points are from the start, so that's why skills around experimentation, prototyping, and pivoting are essential for intrapreneurs. Sure, some intrapreneurs spend time creating complex systems maps, but most of the intrapreneurs we've met simply got started by learning through doing. An easy way to start is to sense the wider systems around you. Spend time observing entrepreneurs and activists to see what solutions are emerging on the margins of the system you want to influence.

Systems Change, Equality, and Equity

Systems change is intricately related to two key concepts in social change. These concepts are "equality" and "equity":

– Equality is about treating everyone the same.

– Equity is about everyone having what they need to be successful.

Equality aims at fairness, but it does not necessarily take into account the fact that people start with different levels of resources. Equity on the other hand assumes different starting positions and takes those differences into account when trying to reform systems. Generally speaking, it is unhelpful to prioritize equality before equity questions have been addressed; if not, we may unwittingly reinforce inequality.

Take the COVID-19 pandemic as an example. The long-term health impacts of the pandemic are still unknown, but even at the time of writing, it is already becoming clear that equality and equity are not the same thing when it comes to essential medical supplies like face masks, disposable medical gloves, and hand sanitizer.

Everyone on the planet has an unambiguously equal right to stay safe from the virus. But do they deserve an equal right to access essential medical supplies given a worldwide shortage of these supplies?

Because some people are structurally more exposed to COVID-19 infection (e.g., frontline medical workers, sanitation workers, bus drivers, grocery store clerks, migrant farm laborers, and people living in urban slums with poor access to water and soap), applying an equity lens would mean these populations should be prioritized first in the distribution of precious medical supplies. As life-protecting supplies become more available, they can be distributed increasingly outward to groups in safer situations, such as high-wage earners who can easily work from home and order groceries online.

Sadly, because essential supplies are currently being distributed to those with the most resources (i.e., money and power and connections), less socially powerful groups are finding themselves disproportionately exposed to the virus. The Cook County medical examiner in Chicago found that although black residents make up less than a third of Chicago residents, they represent 70 percent of the city's COVID-19 deaths. Black residents are statistically overrepresented in low-wage essential jobs like janitorial service and cooking. They also have historically poorer access to health care, which means they are coming into the COVID-19 pandemic with higher underlying rates of diabetes, high blood pressure, and coronary disease that exacerbates the virus' impact.[18]

So, if at first glance, an equal solution seems to fit because, as in a pandemic, "we are all in this together," we invite you to take a deeper look. What are the inequities in the system you are trying to address and how can your solution account for those to deliver just and sustainable outcomes?

Fig. 4. Illustration from the Interaction Institute for Social Change helps demonstrate the difference between equality and equity. Created by Interaction Institute for Social Change | Artist: Angus Maguire. Adapted by Tom Jennings. http://interactioninstitute.org/illustrating-equality-vs-equity.

TOM FARRAND ON MASS COLLABORATION
FOR SYSTEMS CHANGE

The UK's The Wild Network was formed to support system innovation by catalyzing a "rewilding childhood" movement focused on reconnecting kids with nature and playing outside. Launched with a feature length documentary film called *Project Wild Thing*, filmmaker David Bond appointed himself the "marketing director for nature."

In the last 30 years, kids' physical roaming areas have shrunk by over 80 percent, and obesity and mental health issues have massively increased in young people over the last 10 years. Many people wanted to get behind a systematic approach to improving childhood. Through a simple call to action to grow #wildtime, the network grew into a broad and diverse collection of 30,000 mothers, fathers, guardians, community workers, activists, policy-makers, doctors, caregivers, creatives, play-workers, and educators. Rounding out the group of individuals were 2,000 organizations and initiatives, ranging from companies to NGOs to hundreds of grassroots projects with interests across nature, education, health, and play.

The Wild Network was bolstered by time, money, access to networks, and other resources from organizations including The National Trust, the Royal Society for the Protection of Birds, Arla Foods, Play England, The Wildlife Trusts, Save the Children, the National Health Service, and others, with Esmée Fairbairn Foundation providing seed funding.

Tom Farrand, a League Catalyst and a member of the founding team for The Wild Network, offered this reflection on the campaign's success:

> "We quickly recognized we didn't have a supply issue, but we had a demand issue and had to find a new way of talking about this challenge, reframing the benefits to make them more appealing to parents and kids across the country. Starting out organically, we invited the growing community to help identify major barriers to keeping children from engaging with nature. They identified four barriers:

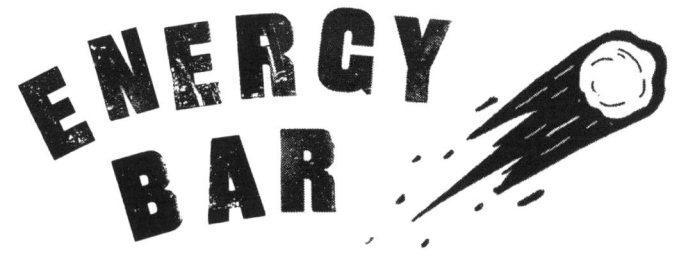

Fear:
Concerns about 'stranger danger' and dangerous
streets, and a generally risk-averse culture

Time:
Time-poor parents, nature-starved curriculum
at school, and a lack of free-range play

Space:
Vanishing green space and commercialization
of play and playspaces

Technology:
Rise of screen time

Through a combination of innovation and campaigning, The
Wild Network continues to tackle the barriers—showcasing
inspiring local solutions on the web platform and social media
channels like Playing Out where people can shut their streets
down for the community to come together for an afternoon,
developing innovations like the Wild Time app with Persil
which gives parents and kids time-based ideas for outdoor play,
and piloting Wild Time Learning, a teaching platform that
links outdoor learning to the school curriculum through lesson
plans."

While the Wild Network community continues to grow and over
one million people have seen *Project Wild Thing*, the challenges are
still numerous and signal that the rewilding movement is still in the
early days of working out how to grow system innovations at scale.
Impact measurement is challenging. The movement competes with
flush media budgets of tech/entertainment brands. Also funding
experimental collaborative efforts in the current economic climate
is tough too.

Commit to Asking a Higher Order Question

Quests start with a question. The etymological root of the word "question" in Latin is *quaerere*, meaning to seek or ask. When you set out on an intrapreneurial journey, you are asking a question that has yet to be posed within the workplace system. Intrapreneurs are seekers looking for answers to big "What if?", "Why?", and "How might we?" questions like:

– How might we bank the unbankable?

– What if we converted our delivery fleets to zero-carbon transport?

– What if we treated people who have experienced domestic abuse as generously as we do people who are homeless due to natural disasters?

– How might we move our charity past seeing the private sector merely as a source of charitable donations?

– What if we provided world-class education for everyone, everywhere?

– How might governments co-create with the very public they are intended to serve to produce more meaningful outcomes?

Answers to powerful questions are not obvious and sometimes take decades or lifetimes to uncover. Before you embark on your intrapreneurial journey, be sure you're asking a question worth investigating. How, you might ask, do you know what's worth investigating?

The "Three Order Question Framework" is used at the School for Social Entrepreneurs Canada's Unlearning Program, a curriculum being developed by League Catalysts Chryssa Koulis and Marjorie Brans. The framework invites innovators to consider their questions through the lens of math equations, helping them identify where a bigger question can be asked.

Take the following three equations:

1. Lowest order: 6 + ___ *= 6*

The "lowest order" equation has only one right answer (which is "zero" for all you math whizzes out there). Many of the sustainability challenges that organizations try to address are asked at a level where the answer needs to fit in an unyielding frame of existing constraints, rules, and resources. It's no wonder that very little changes when questions about how to make the workplace fairer or supply chains greener must fit in the blank space of the current system.

Example: How do we green our [environmentally destructive] company by getting employees to turn off the lights and print on both sides of paper [while continuing to produce environmentally destructive products]?

2. Higher order: ___ *+* ___ *= 6*

In contrast to the single answer of the lowest order question, a "higher order" question opens up a second variable and thus allows for an infinite number of answers. The sum of six can be obtained using positive integers, negative and positive numbers, fractions, and possibly exponents, square roots, imaginary numbers, and so on (we'll leave the solution set to the real math geniuses). Intrapreneurial quests that are framed around two open variables allow for many new possibilities to emerge.

Example: How does our company produce products and services that at minimum, don't harm the environment, and may even improve it?

3. Highest order: ___ *+* ___ *=* ___

The highest order questions are game changers that do not impose any hard constraints.

Example: How might we tap into our historic leadership as a company to help our country leapfrog into the green economy?

A common maxim is that "creativity loves constraints." Sometimes too much freedom is overwhelming and it becomes difficult to know where to start. There's value in asking the highest order questions in that they can stimulate whole new fields and disciplines to explore, but realize that you may need to answer intermediate "higher" order questions in the interim.

Note that the "Three Order Question Framework" roughly corresponds to McKinsey & Company's "Three Horizons" concept of innovation. In this model, the first horizon involves business as usual. The second horizon involves change that is more modest, but is more immediately attainable given that it is found in adjacent territory (like a chrysalis and its relationship to a caterpillar). The third horizon involves transformative change that does not have any seeming relationship to what currently exists (like a butterfly's relationship to a caterpillar).[19]

For instance, in reference to the era of horse and buggies, Henry Ford is famously (but dubiously) quoted as saying, "If I had asked people what they wanted, they would have said faster horses."[20] Horizon one competitors to Henry Ford may not have been tinkering with equine DNA, but they were certainly looking for ways to improve buggy sales. Horizon two competitors may have sought to improve the design of carriages so that they could travel faster. Ford radically shifted the world to horizon three by transforming transportation with his system of producing cars for the masses. Eventually, Ford's horizon three became horizon one and was overtaken by a long stream of other horizon three thinkers.

If you're just getting started in intrapreneurship, you'll probably want to start with a good higher order question and save the highest order questions for later. On the other hand, if you're already at the stage where you can jump to horizon three, more power to you! Note, we return to the Three Horizons model in Chapter Four.

MARJORIE BRANS ON HIGHER ORDER QUESTIONS

If you are able to generate a powerful higher order question, you might unlock something surprising. To illustrate, League Catalyst Marjorie Brans offered this example from a project she recently worked on at a dance service organization:

"I was asked for help on a project aimed at moving away from privileging only European forms of dance like ballet and Western contemporary dance. The organization's members found the issue contentious, even while recognizing that it was no longer acceptable that Indigenous, South Asian, hip hop, and other forms of dance were not garnering the resources they needed to thrive. The issue was that the ballet and contemporary dancers were already making poverty wages and it was hard to justify spreading very thin resources across even more dancers.

I realized that the association had a math problem. They were asking the lowest order question, 'How might we pay all our dancers fairly with such a paltry budget?,' assuming the answer had to fit within the existing constraints of current resources. A higher order question could be, 'How might we generate more resources through a new social enterprise or new corporate sponsorship?' I thought that was all well and good, but wondered if an even higher order question could be asked.

This is when I began to wonder, 'Why do people dance in the first place?' The answer seemed obvious and not worth stating, but I insisted on an answer. The response from the team was, 'It's an important form of human expression and a way to make sense of the world.'

Well, in that answer lay an intriguing idea, 'Who cares about human expression? Why would anyone with money care to finance it?' My mind immediately jumped to artificial intelligence (AI) companies. As more people accuse them of taking humans out of the economic picture, never before has human expression and sense-making been so important. In fact, the more diverse human expression and sense-making are, the better. I suggested the dance organization pilot a partnership between the AI sector and human artists to find opportunities for mutual gain. Dance and other art forms could help AI companies explore the human implications of this new technology through the creative commentary of artists. Meanwhile, artists could be paid for this work. Dreaming up something even wilder, perhaps AI companies could be required to contribute a small equity share in their companies to the cultural sector. As the new technology grows, cultural sense-making could grow alongside it. Indeed, an exploratory project inspired by these ideas is underway now."

Planning Your Route

Once you have your system-challenging higher order question, you'll need to identify a world-changing idea that might be an answer to that question. In a nutshell, a world-changing idea sits at the intersection of societal need, a business or entrepreneurial opportunity, and your values and gifts.

Ask yourself:

- **Am I addressing a real problem that needs solving?**
  The League of Intrapreneurs uses the United Nations (UN) Sustainable Development Goals (SDGs) as a framework for impact, which can help to identify universal areas of need (examined more on page 124). Systems change theory, discussed above, is also helpful in focusing your efforts on the highest points of potential impact.

- **Is this a new and fresh approach? And is there the potential for sustainability, replication, and scale?**
  Remember, as an intrapreneur you are working for an organization that has an existing set of priorities and focus areas. How might your idea address a pain point or help achieve a strategic priority for your organization?

- **Does this idea align with the unique set of values and gifts that my team and I bring to the world?**
  Changing the world can be tricky business, so ensuring your idea taps into your strengths and aligns with your values will increase the likelihood of success. It will also ensure you show up with authenticity and credibility, tipping the scales in your favor.

If you answered yes to these questions, you're potentially on to a world-changing idea.

Note that you may only have a clear sense of one or two of these elements—that's okay. Many intrapreneurs start with one element and expand their viewpoint over time to include the others (see the Energy Bar on the next page for an example of how this process can proceed in stages). The idea usually comes after a great deal of immersion in the issue area and time to see what pieces of the puzzle are missing.

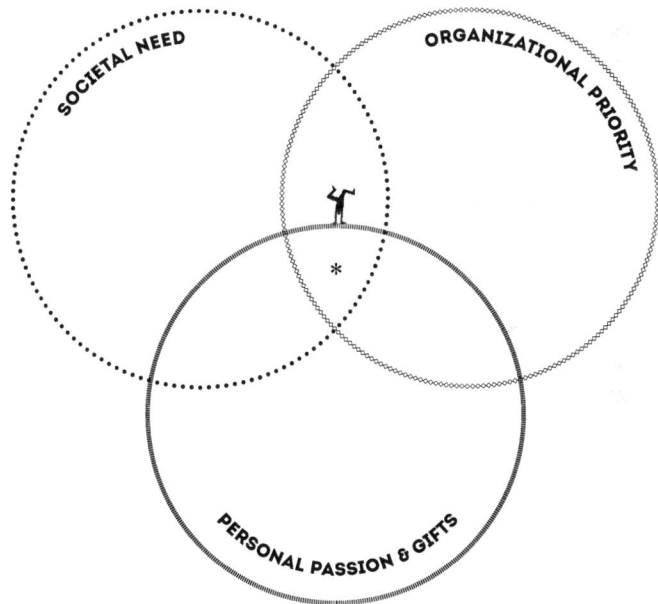

* Your North Star

Fig. 5. Find your world-changing idea where societal need, organizational priority, and your values and gifts meet.

SAIDAH NASH CARTER ON STARTING
WITH A SHARED LOVE OF AFRICA

Eighty percent of the African workforce makes a living from agriculture, but many face hindrances to growth due to a lack of access to capital. How can data and technology be used to give banks the confidence to lend to farmers with no credit profile?

This is the question intrapreneur Saidah Nash Carter was asking at Thomson Reuters in South Africa when she developed the Bankable Farmer initiative. Bankable Farmer combines advanced data science approaches, alternative data sets, and a novel approach to risk modeling to enable traditional banks to lend to small commercial farmers across Africa.

This big vision, as Saidah explains, started with a conversation over dinner.

> "I was working at Thomson Reuters and was invited to a partner event with Vodafone in 2013. I sat next to Shannon Lucas—another 'dyed in the wool' intrapreneur. We started talking about personal interests and things that got us going and we discovered an interest in Africa was something we had in common. Working in Africa was not in our day job descriptions, but we were both interested in the continent.

> We decided to explore if there was something we could do together. We knew our companies were partners, so maybe there was something there. We also liked each other. I think this is something people often overlook. It's important that you like the people you work with, especially if you are working on hard stuff. It makes the journey that much more enjoyable.

> When we went back to our companies we realized that Africa was a continent of strategic interest to them. So, this gave us a platform to marry our personal interests with the strategic objectives of our companies.

We then began the creation of a joint value proposition.

If we were one company in Africa, what would we do? What were we good at and how would we contribute uniquely to creating something of value? Thomson Reuters has deep banking domain expertise as well as in the delivery of data and packaging of data. Vodafone has a mobile technology platform. So, we identified clear lanes where we could deliver value.

Next, we designed a series of innovation workshops with our joint customers (banks). It took us a year to get all the right people in the room. And what we heard is that banks were interested in agricultural supply chains—particularly small farmers. They saw an opportunity to expand their markets to serve these customers, but they had no idea how to do this.

That was the original kernel for what eventually evolved into Bankable Farmer. We knew there was an opportunity there because these super competitive banks were interested in expanding into the rest of Africa and leveraging newer technologies to be able to do so.

We then talked to farmers in Rwanda, which was a real turning point for us. It validated a lot of our assumptions about the need for access to capital. We then worked with academic and NGO partners to further understand the market opportunity and validate the need and opportunity space."

Picturing the Implementation of Your Idea:
Your Route and Destination

With your world-changing idea might come a vague sense of how you'll implement it and cause the change to happen. A Theory of Change is a methodology for action planning and evaluation that is used heavily in philanthropic, non-profit, and government sectors to promote social change. A Theory of Change defines long-term goals and then maps backward to identify necessary preconditions.

Identifying these preconditions is critical or you may end up wasting resources. In his book *Questions Are the Answer*, author Hal Gregersen describes the #monkeyfirst principle at X, a subsidiary of Alphabet, the parent company of Google. X exists to solve "age-old, world-hurting problems." Given the inherent difficulty of the problems at X, employees are naturally tempted to list the easiest tasks first and the hardest ones last. Tackling the easy tasks first is a great way for people to gain a sense of progress. But that's not necessarily the best strategy.

A common hashtag around the office at X is #monkeyfirst.

The monkey refers to a fictitious project to get a monkey to sit on top of a pole and recite Shakespeare. Without identifying all the preconditions for success, X employees are likely to overlook the fact that if they don't get a monkey to speak in Elizabethan era poetry, they might as well forget erecting the pole.[21]

In short, specifying a goal and envisioning the entire journey is important. Say you have the intention to grow the market share of your company's new socially beneficial product in two years.

How will you increase the number of retailers? Or increase the amount that current retailers sell? Avoid putting yourself in the unattractive position of having to revise your projections downward. Come up with a Theory of Change so that your assumptions for the whole duration of the quest are mapped out.

As you develop your Theory of Change, channel Merlin. You may recall Merlin as the legendary wizard who served King Arthur. In *The Once and Future King*, author T. H. White portrayed the wizard as someone who could move back through time. With these magical powers, he could "remember the future."

Note that you may only have a clear sense of one or two of these elements—that's okay. Many intrapreneurs start with one element and expand their viewpoint over time to include the others. The idea usually comes after a great deal of immersion in the issue area and time to see what pieces of the puzzle are missing.

Remembering the future requires you to see:

– How you got there

– When you achieved the goal

– What "halfway" to the goal looked like—what tasks had already been completed and what remained to be done

The further we cast our mental map backwards from the future, the closer we get to current day and clarity on what must be achieved now to get started.[22]

To offer an example that is (slightly) less fantastical than a poetry-reciting monkey, take Jessy Kate Schlinger. Jessy Kate was an engineer at NASA when she was invited to join a conference hosted by the UN to explore how humans could move into outer space and live on the moon or planets like Mars. What intrigued her most wasn't the focus on the technological innovation required for such an audacious vision, but the social systems that humans would need to innovate to survive and thrive beyond the Earth's atmosphere. Inspired by that question, she left and established Embassy Networks, a network of co-living spaces around the US prototyping collaborative living. While most work in the area of space exploration is focused on technical matters like the most advanced rockets, rover vehicles, and mini nuclear reactors (all Shakespeare-reciting monkeys for sure), Jessy Kate is focused on other monkeys like how people can live together harmoniously in unconventional arrangements.

As you remember the future of intrapreneurial success at your organization, you'll want to investigate how the preconditions for change get realized. How has change happened in the past? Who needs to be involved? When? How do you expect to overcome institutional inertia, hierarchy, and "carry on" incentives? How will you bring along people who derive security from playing by the rules and dislike disruptions to business as usual?

Be sure to leave a few blank spaces in your mental map for the people, places, and situations you don't know about yet. You're likely to encounter the so-called "unknown unknowns." That's what happened in 1492 when Christopher Columbus set sail toward Asia but famously "found" America (which had already been occupied for well over 10,000 years). Until his death, he remained convinced that he had found Asia. According to Chris Kutarna, author of *The Age of Discovery*, Columbus' mental map was based on a Biblical story that Noah had three sons who had given birth to three races of Man—Africa, Asia, and Europe:

> "That was humanity. That was the world, full stop. His mental map prevented Columbus from making sense of his own

discovery. It's why 'America' isn't named after Columbus, but after Amerigo Vespucci. Amerigo was the Italian explorer who, some 10 years after Columbus' voyages, popularized the insight that the lands Columbus had found were, in fact, a *mundus novus*. A new world. By helping Europeans to make that mental shift, Amerigo unleashed Europe's capacity to navigate that new world—for good and ill."[23]

Indeed, many of the world's current ills trace their roots to the negative legacy of this colonial mentality. But the point we are making here is that your colleagues may make and encounter all sorts of 21st century "discoveries" (more positive than land and people to exploit), but, until they update their mental maps, they may not be able to make sense of their significance.

Your job as an intrapreneur is to help them update their mental maps and to keep blank spaces in your own as you encounter the 21st century's equivalent of new territory, flora, and fauna. After all, we have no idea what awaits us at the end of the path. In case it is not obvious, the notion of social and environmental sustainability is not a fixed point on a map; it is a horizon in the distance that our species strives to reach. As long as you can recognize the destination when you reach the desired end state, all you need to do is fill in the missing elements on the map and remember how you got there.

Take Airbnb as an example. Who would have thought much of it 10 years ago? The model was dismissed by many as a niche or a fad. But today, Airbnb and its sharing economy model are disrupting industries from automotive to finance. Company managers have had to clear space in their mental map from one of exclusively making products for people to own to one that includes platforms for sharing and access.

ABYSS of CYNICISM

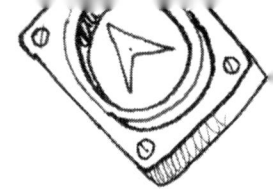

Staying on Track with Natural Navigation and a Compass

The earliest humans who roamed the Earth did so without the aid of any device. Through careful observation and pattern recognition, these explorers oriented themselves using features of the landscape to establish location, direction, distance traveled, and even a likely weather forecast.

Natural navigation expert and educator Tristan Gooley explains that "everything outdoors is a clue. Every plant, animal, cloud or star is both a sign and part of our map."[24] For instance, rainbows can help you orient yourself and predict the weather. All rainbows involve three elements: the sun behind us, the rain in front of us, and us as an observer in the middle. Extending the arc of a rainbow into an imaginary circle, we can locate the sun precisely opposite the "antisolar point" found at the center of the circle. With this information in hand, we can also determine the direction of our travel. Combined with the knowledge that weather systems typically come from the west, we can further surmise that if we see a rainbow in the morning, we're likely to get rained on, but in the afternoon, we're likely to encounter dry skies.[25]

Learning what natural clues mean requires a lifetime of study, and in the same way, intrapreneurs develop the capacity to read workplace clues through experience. For instance, if a new executive director joins and changes the office layout, this may signal their need to exercise power visibly. Perhaps, they may even take over the biggest and most prominently positioned office. The intrapreneur now knows that future proposals may garner more support if they offer the executive director a chance to be seen publicly as a powerful person.

The skill of natural navigation will take time to develop. You're likely to misread the clues at first, so if you're just starting out, look for mentors who can help teach you what clues to look for and what they might mean.

As you move through the intrapreneurial terrain, also remember that because the human body favors a dominant eye, most, if not all, humans traveling long distances tend to veer slightly to the left or right of a straight line. For example, if your team favors business analysis over social and environmental impact or vice versa, you risk losing sight of important goals. The deviation won't be noticeable over a short stretch, but may cause you to travel in circles if you venture out long enough.

Even the best natural navigators would do well to obtain the *Intrapreneur's Compass* (found on the League's website). The *Compass* can help you stay the course and guide you when you realize you're lost or there are few clues to orient you. Compasses work by pointing the traveler to the cardinal directions, north in the Northern Hemisphere and south in the Southern Hemisphere. Similarly the *Intrapreneur's Compass* has points that serve as guardrails to ensure you don't navigate off the side of a cliff. These guardrails take into account important things like your "higher order question," your motivation, current travel conditions, and your plan to stay resilient.

Be clear from the start about your initiative's non-negotiables and don't compromise on these. In fact, clearly communicate these non-negotiables from the start and document them for future reference. For instance, you might not accept project outcomes that don't result in a tangible reduction in greenhouse gases (versus simply raising awareness of climate change). Or you might insist that your project be deemed a positive contribution to social equity not only by your corporation, but also by a wide group of erstwhile critics. Or you might not accept any project outcome that comes at too great a mental health cost to your team. Whatever your non-negotiables are, make them clear up front and document them so that they can serve as compass guardrails when you're deep into your journey.

Regularly check your project bearings against your non-negotiables. At the first sign that your team may be losing its way, raise your concerns. You can show what changes are needed and distill concrete actions to restore your project's mission. If something is a direct threat to your goals, engage in the necessary conversations.

"Whatever your personal beliefs and experiences, I invite you to consider that we need a new worldview to navigate this chaotic time.

We cannot hope to make sense using our old maps. It won't help to dust them off or reprint them in bold colors.

The more we rely on them, the more disoriented we become. They cause us to focus on the wrong things and blind us to what's significant. Using them, we will journey only to greater chaos."

MARGARET J. WHEATLEY,
LEADERSHIP AND THE NEW SCIENCE:
DISCOVERING ORDER IN A CHAOTIC WORLD

QUESTIONS TO ASK YOURSELF
What's their story?
What's mine?
Who can I get on board?

3

Enrolling Your Co-Travelers

Humans love stories about heroes. No wonder Marvel Studios has released more than 20 superhero movies to great commercial success. In social innovation, hero-preneurship can be a seductive narrative, but in reality, no one can move a large institution or system alone. To be effective agents of change, we have to find others to share the burden, risk, and rewards.

Successful intrapreneurship is not about beating out your colleagues or defending against their resistance to your ideas. Intrapreneurs who try to be heroes burn out quickly, or they get fired for irritating too many people. Entrenched organizational culture can be a powerful opponent, and the best intrapreneurs humble themselves before it.

Recognize that you're taking on a difficult task when you point over a ridge to a future horizon and tell naysayers to trust and follow you. The task is even more difficult when you're tackling issues that aren't connected to the organization's currently defined mission and strategy, or in ways that challenge the accepted ways of operating. Beyond making the usual rational, logical "business case" for any initiative you've been trained to do in your job, you'll need to bring additional emotional, social, and cultural approaches to your communication and persuasion plan.

Storytelling is the foundation of persuasion and recruiting people to your cause.

It Starts with Stories

Facts are facts; the stories we tell ourselves tell us what the facts mean. When we make decisions "rationally," we try to shape our beliefs and actions to reason and facts. But, the last decade's explosion of behavioral economics units in governments and businesses around the world is a testament to something we all knew intuitively: humans are not very rational.

Emotional, social, and cultural factors as well as psychological and cognitive tendencies equally—if not predominantly—come into play when we are making decisions. Stories have a lot to do with what we deem a fact, which facts we see as relevant to a given issue, and who possesses facts (i.e., who is a credible expert). In other words, stories that are cultivated in a particular culture provide the frame through which we determine what is or is not relevant in a given picture.

If a workplace culture says that personal emotions or the impact of work decisions on an employee's family fall "out of the frame of materiality," then the fact that you are sad or that you have to miss your child's school play to stay late at the office will be considered irrelevant.

This is not to say that facts and reason do not matter, but more that stories do a lot of the hard work first. In "Why Facts Don't Change Our Minds," Elizabeth Kolbert cites a study that found something you have probably noticed: people employ rational logic when they have a high motivation to investigate or get involved in a matter.[26] Otherwise, they rely on social cues and what they think everyone around them already knows. If the so-called "facts" that you present aren't in the social frame, they are likely to be dismissed or not heard.

One of your primary jobs as an intrapreneur is to help reset the frame—to shift the view of what is salient or valued by your colleagues and key stakeholders. To do this will require telling new stories to counter the current narrative that more often than not blocks people's imaginations or will to make a change.

First, you need to know your own story from your position within the system. For inspiration, look to League Fellow Ryan Shepard. Ryan works as an intrapreneur for CARE, a 75-year-old NGO that works in 95 countries around the world with the primary objective of alleviating poverty and advancing social justice. He is leading the development of a Global Innovation Hub to leverage CARE's resources and global reach to create pathways for new ideas in collaboration with new partners and communities. He understands that his personal story is key to his effectiveness:

> "I believe that power comes from having a deep understanding of your own narrative and its relation to the world around you. You have to look inward and understand who you are, what your values are and what really matters to you, and then take the very scary step, a non-self-centered step, and try to deeply understand others and the conditions and circumstances in the world around you. If you find ways where those two things come together, then you become powerful and become part of something that starts to be bigger than you.
>
> This is particularly relevant in the development space. There is often a temptation to try 'saving' people from the global south. The reality is that we can all learn a lot from each other. More importantly, we have to be courageous if we hope to address the systems that lead to great inequity, rather than providing band-aids for the symptoms. This requires collaboration and a values-driven approach that delivers human-centered outcomes."

Once upon a cold, lonely knight … long long ago …

REFRAMING THE NARRATIVE

What do public figures Alexandria Ocasio-Cortez, Donald Trump, Greta Thunberg, and Martin Luther King Jr. have in common? For better or worse, all have demonstrated a knack for resetting a narrative and changing the terms of debate. Let's take the example of Martin Luther King's famous "Letter from a Birmingham Jail." He penned the missive as a response to eight white local clergymen who had, in an open letter, criticized "outsiders" to Birmingham, Alabama. Specifically they chided activists like King for engaging in civil rights demonstrations, instead of using the courts to press their case. Here is an excerpt of King's letter dated April 16, 1963[27]:

> "My Dear Fellow Clergymen: While confined here in the Birmingham city jail, I came across your recent statement calling my present activities 'unwise and untimely'... Since I feel that you are men of genuine good will and that your criticisms are sincerely set forth, I want to try to answer your statement in what I hope will be patient and reasonable terms.
>
> I think I should indicate why I am here in Birmingham, since you have been influenced by the view which argues against 'outsiders coming in.' I have the honor of serving as president of the Southern Christian Leadership Conference, an organization operating in every southern state, with headquarters in Atlanta, Georgia ... Several months ago the affiliate here in Birmingham asked us to be on call to engage in a nonviolent direct action program if such were deemed necessary ... But more basically, I am in Birmingham because injustice is here ...
>
> Moreover, I am cognizant of the interrelatedness of all communities and states ... We are caught in an inescapable network of mutuality, tied in a single garment of destiny. Whatever affects one directly, affects all indirectly ...
>
> You deplore the demonstrations taking place in Birmingham. But your statement, I am sorry to say, fails to express a similar concern for the conditions that brought about the demonstrations. I am sure that none of you would want to rest content with the superficial kind of social analysis that deals merely with effects

ENERGY BAR

and does not grapple with underlying causes. It is unfortunate that demonstrations are taking place in Birmingham, but it is even more unfortunate that the city's white power structure left the Negro community with no alternative.

You may well ask: 'Why direct action? Why sit ins, marches and so forth? Isn't negotiation a better path?' You are quite right in calling for negotiation. Indeed, this is the very purpose of direct action. Nonviolent direct action seeks to create such a crisis and foster such a tension that a community which has constantly refused to negotiate is forced to confront the issue. It seeks so to dramatize the issue that it can no longer be ignored ...

We know through painful experience that freedom is never voluntarily given by the oppressor; it must be demanded by the oppressed. Frankly, I have yet to engage in a direct action campaign that was 'well timed' in the view of those who have not suffered unduly from the disease of segregation. For years now I have heard the word 'Wait!' It rings in the ear of every Negro with piercing familiarity. This 'Wait' has almost always meant 'Never.' We must come to see, with one of our distinguished jurists, that 'justice too long delayed is justice denied.' ...

One may well ask: 'How can you advocate breaking some laws and obeying others?' The answer lies in the fact that there are two types of laws: just and unjust. I would be the first to advocate obeying just laws. One has not only a legal but a moral responsibility to obey just laws. Conversely, one has a moral responsibility to disobey unjust laws. I would agree with St. Augustine that 'an unjust law is no law at all.'"

King's letter has become famous because it deftly rejects a narrative of moderation that seems reasonable to the casual observer, but that King argues is deeply problematic. He points to a politically naked truth that "freedom is never voluntarily given by the oppressor" and that calls for activists to use the courts do not recognize the deeply unjust legal system in the United States. In the next section, we deconstruct King's letter step by step.

Constructing a Compelling Narrative

Facts and stories need to weave together in a seductive mix that persuades key stakeholders to heed your call to action. Some people are natural storytellers, but most of us need a little help to construct a compelling narrative.

In this section, we'll help you figure out how to gather everyone around the proverbial campfire where you can mesmerize your colleagues with a story that captures their imaginations.

Identifying and Understanding the Current Narrative

Before constructing a counter-narrative, you'll want to articulate the current organizational narrative about the issue your project is tackling. It might be something like, "that matter sits over there and has nothing to do with us," or, "that matter is under control and we don't have a problem." Whatever the narrative is, you'll want to analyze it thoroughly.

Based on approaches developed by the Center for Story-Based Strategies with adaptations we've made for the purposes of the Guide, we suggest the following steps while using Martin Luther King Jr.'s example to illustrate the points.[28]

1. Identify the *background assumptions* of the story (e.g., outsiders have no business in Birmingham; social grievances should be handled in court and through negotiation; and people must obey all laws).

2. Identify what *we have to believe to believe that the current narrative is true* (e.g., injustice in one community is unrelated to injustice in another; the courts can handle this matter effectively; the country's laws are just).

3. Identify the *standard for rationality* that applies in the story (e.g., a person's identity as an outsider is more important than the truth of their message; unjust order is more important than direct action and justice; we should obey laws even those that are unjust).

4. Identify *how the story makes existing outcomes possible or inevitable* (e.g., "whatever affects one [community] directly, affects all indirectly"; "justice too long delayed is justice denied").

5. Identify *fissures* or cracks in the story (e.g., "one has a moral responsibility to disobey unjust laws. I would agree with St. Augustine that 'an unjust law is no law at all.'"). Apply pressure to fissures where the story is particularly vulnerable, already in the process of changing, or extra-valuable as leverage. King borrows the influence and prominence of St. Augustine to press his case among other religious figures who are less likely to dismiss this Biblical scholar than a "rabble-rousing" black minister.

The story elements that King chose to include or omit determine the shape and size of the frame of relevance and show where the frame can be broken to allow in facts and emotions that fall outside the current frame.

Developing a Counter-Narrative

Once you have analyzed the dominant story, your team can construct an alternative version that builds bridges to future possibilities. The FRAMES Approach, also developed by the Center for Story-Based Strategies and adapted here for intrapreneurs, offers a step-by-step guide to do so.

FRAMES stands for:

Frame-Reframe-Accessible-Memorable-Emotional-Simple.[29]

F. Frame the Issue

Frame a problem as an opportunity. Where others see challenges or constraints, you see barriers to innovate around and against. Some call this skill "integrative thinking." We like to think of it as generative thinking. Good framing means defining the problem, who will be broadly impacted, and the solution in ways that are consistent with your project's vision and values.

Taci Abreu, FARM Rio's Marketing Director whom we introduced earlier, wanted to convince others on her team to reduce waste by making clothes out of leftover materials. She knew the dominant story at FARM was one of beauty and trends, and that there was a risk that reused material could be seen as something "less than." So, instead of just selling the idea of using less fabric, she designed a dress. She showed through a prototype how waste reduction through reuse of material could be both beautiful and trendy and offer new market opportunities. As the Marketing Director, she knew she could offer a compelling counter-narrative that addressed her colleagues' fears head-on by bringing to life beautiful clothing made from scraps.

R. Reframe the Old Story & Communicate A New One

Be careful that your message is not just reiterating the old frame. Reframing means changing the terms of debate on the issue. The alternative story must challenge the underlying assumptions of the current story, taking care to avoid accidentally reinforcing them.

Scott Summitt, an industrial designer and founder of Bespoke Innovation, endeavored to reframe the narrative around prosthetic limbs.[30] After doing research with prostheses users, Summitt discovered that many were embarrassed and tried to conceal their artificial limbs. He saw an opportunity to reframe the problem by presenting prosthetic limbs as a fashion accessory. His counter-narrative avoided getting mired in functional and medical arguments. Instead, his narrative promoted prostheses, a necessary medical device, as a way for users to express themselves and something they could be proud to show. Based on that premise, Bespoke uses 3-D printing to create prosthetic limbs in different patterns and materials custom to its user. By reframing his customers' problem and presenting a fresh narrative, Summitt was able to innovate a product and engage users.

A. Accessible to the Audience

Customize your message based on who you are trying to persuade. What purpose do they bring to the workplace? How do they think about the issue you're raising? Be as specific as possible about the audience and ensure that the message is crafted in terms of language, context, and values that will be appealing to them (see page 78 on Moral Foundations Theory). If you know that your industry is thinking about your sustainability challenge, you might link your project to the trends and concerns being discussed. Help conservative colleagues see that change is needed just to "keep up with the Joneses" and show conservative stakeholders that the approach has been tried before and is only an extension of what your organization stands for or already does.

 Memorable

People can only process so much information and many of us feel overloaded. So amidst meeting notes, agendas, emails, and PowerPoint presentations, how do you really get people to remember your message? You'll want your message to be "sticky," so that future emotions, experiences, and facts are drawn there and begin to collect critical mass in a counter-narrative. In *Made to Stick: Why Some Ideas Survive and Others Die*, authors Chip and Dan Heath show how simple, unexpected, concrete, credible, and emotional stories get stuck in people's memories.[31] Consider encapsulating your message in a symbol, slogan, or metaphor that captures the essence.

A simple, yet effective way to build bridges to the future is to create a fake press release or news article. You can do this with even the simplest of word processing or presentation software. Identify a publication that has high credibility with your audience and mock up a news article or press release from the future. What would the article or release say about your company if your idea takes off? What impact will it have on the business, customers, and the world? How might your senior leadership team be recognized?

When Gib Bulloch, founder of Accenture Development Partners (ADP), had the idea for a "not-for-loss" consultancy arm of Accenture, he knew he had to do something different to make his case. First, he went straight to senior leadership in the UK, taking a big risk to engage high-level colleagues who could shoot down his idea from the get-go. Then, he created a compelling new narrative: "I sent a fake press article in the *Financial Times* to the Chairman of our board, presenting a couple page spread explaining the concept for ADP. I didn't know him personally, but I knew if I was going to get this off the ground, I needed this level of support." Fortunately for Gib, the Chairman met him for breakfast and ADP was born.

Sometimes being memorable comes from having a conversation in a unique or significant setting. Rather than pitch someone in a meeting room, go for a walk with them or visit a museum together. Getting people outside of the office may encourage their receptivity to your ideas because they will be in a more relaxed and open frame of mind. Other times, presenting striking visuals or prototypes that are unexpected communication tools can get people engaged and help them remember you and your idea.

"A picture is worth a thousand words ... a good prototype is worth a thousand pictures," according to Tom Kelley, co-founder of IDEO.[32] A prototype is a rough model of something you are trying to create. Bringing your idea to life through a tangible prototype is one of the most effective ways to help people see future possibilities.

Thando Moutlana was working at SABMiller, a multinational brewing company in South Africa, when she was struck by inspiration. She wanted to use the spent grain from the company's brewing process to produce nutritious bread that could feed families on low incomes in the communities in which SABMiller was operating. She had received permission from the head of brewing operations to run an experiment, but she needed to rally more internal support for her idea. So, what did she do? She baked. Working with university scientists and a London-based baker to craft a beautiful loaf of bread, she shared the product at a company pitch event.

As people smelled and sampled the bread, they could literally taste the opportunity for SABMiller to have impact while also addressing a business need around waste.

E. Emotional

People don't swing into action because of a pie chart. Gandhi wasn't a charismatic leader because he knew his way around Excel. Rather, through rousing calls-to-action such as the famous "Quit India" speech of 1942, he tapped into people's deeply rooted sense of justice.[33] An effective message should speak to people in terms of values and deliver soul-stirring impact. Emotional responses come from stories that involve tragedy, hope, anger, frustration, and joy.

Much of the art of persuasion boils down to being authentic, so help your audience understand who you are. Don't be afraid to get personal as Yun Hui Hong of eBay Korea did when she proposed a specialized online store that would cater to the needs of people with disabilities. Yun Hui could describe this challenge firsthand because childhood cancer resulted in paralysis of her daughter (read more about Yun Hui's innovation in Chapter Five).

People love stories about other people. Introducing a protagonist (or protagonists) in your story can bring an abstract concept out of the ether and into reality. It can help people relate to your idea on a more emotional level. Mechanical things (e.g., memoranda of understanding, scopes of work, intellectual property agreements, project plans, etc.) will help clarify your plan and approach, but nothing can replace human connections.

For example, when Milana Momcilovic started her social intrapreneurship venture with the aim of integrating social entrepreneurship into the procurement processes of Coca-Cola Hellenic Bottling Company, she made it personal. She knew that a big barrier to uptake was the lack of understanding about social entrepreneurship and how creating social impact was possible without requiring additional corporate investment.

"During my pitch meeting, I explained to the audience that simply by having their lunch today they had provided income for five people with special needs and contributed to the meals of 10 elderly people. How? I had worked with the person overseeing the lunch break to order catering from 'Kitchen on Wheels,' a local social enterprise that prepares and delivers food and has a dual social mission: employing people with special needs and ensuring each meal purchased from them for full price subsidizes one meal for an elderly person who cannot cook for themselves. Through this experience and being introduced to the people they were benefiting (protagonists), my audience could better visualize the potential impact of social procurement, and understand the benefits for the company and the positive impact it would create for the community. Overall, they were much more open to my project proposal."

S. Simple & Short

Sometimes, your passion and excitement will scare people. The more ambitious the change you envision, the more people will hear that you're upsetting order. Most people are invested in keeping things the same, or at least within the realm of the familiar. Gifford Pinchot III, League Advisor and the person who coined the term "intrapreneurship," says, "If you make your project seem too world changing, they will respond with delaying tactics and requests for more information. This does not move your project forward."[34] Therefore, you'll want to communicate but not over-communicate. Think about spoon-feeding your plan if you're serving elephant for dinner.

ENERGY BAR

MYRIAM SIDIBE ON REFRAMING PROFIT
AS A POWERFUL FORCE FOR GOOD

Myriam Sidibe has a PhD in public health with a specific focus on handwashing with soap. A likely career journey for someone in her field would have been to work for a UN agency or NGO. But, Myriam chose to work for Unilever—because she felt she could have a greater impact on health outcomes by harnessing the power of her employer's global brand.

Myriam went to work initially for the Lifebuoy soap brand because one of the simplest and most effective solutions to preventing disease, such as influenza, SARS, and cholera, is handwashing with soap. To help unlock the potential of the Lifebuoy brand, she needed to construct a narrative that helped corporate teams to see beyond short-term numbers and units sold to longer-term opportunities to save lives.

To do this, she reminded the team at Unilever of their heritage making soap for medicinal purposes: Lifebuoy was founded in Victorian England in 1894 to combat cholera. She showed them how their expertise in marketing was one of the most important ingredients in health outcomes. They could help translate scientific facts into tangible purchase decisions—in this case, buying and using soap. And, finally, she showed the direct links between sales and lives saved. She helped people to find purpose in profit. Today her intrapreneurial team has reached nearly 200 million people with messages about handwashing with soap and is transforming health outcomes around the world.

"I think this drive for profit is extremely powerful.

Sometimes more powerful than the most committed charity or government ... to make handwashing a daily habit requires sustained funding to refine this behavior. In short, those that fight for public health are actually dependent upon the soap companies to keep promoting handwashing with soap."

Framing & Moral Foundations

As you consider reframing the dominant narrative to support your new idea, you will need to account for the specific worldviews of your audience. Each of us brings our lived experiences, values, and worldviews to work with us each day, and these inform the decisions we make. While worldviews will be unique to each individual and culture, researchers have found that there are broad categories of worldviews or moral foundations that cut across cultures and geographies.

Moral Foundations Theory, developed by a group of social and cultural psychologists, advances the idea that there are five to six innate and universal building blocks of any human group's—and by extension, any individual human's—system of morality.[35]

Using these foundational concepts, "each culture then constructs virtues, narratives, and institutions on top of these foundations, thereby creating the unique moralities we see around the world, and conflicting within nations too." Around the world, moral systems in different countries develop across a conservative to liberal spectrum. The details from country to country may differ, but there are always camps of "conservative" versus "liberal" groups in any large human group, however that is defined in a specific context.

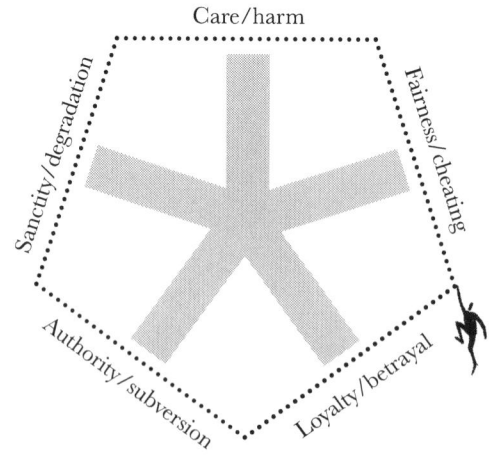

The five foundational concepts are:

Care/harm:

This building block relates to the human capacity for empathy and to the virtues of kindness, gentleness, and nurturance

Fairness/cheating:

This building block relates to ideas of justice, rights, and autonomy. The research team is quick to point out that the concept of equality is not necessarily linked to the idea of fairness in all moral systems, as equality is favored by social liberals, whereas "proportionality" is endorsed by both liberals and conservatives.

Loyalty/betrayal:

This building block relates to virtues of patriotism and self- sacrifice in favor of our in-group in a "one for all, and all for one" mentality.

Authority/subversion:

This building block relates to our long primate history of hierarchical social interactions with emphasis on the virtues of leadership and followership, including deference to legitimate authority and respect for traditions.

Sanctity/degradation:

This building block relates to ideas around cultivating life that is elevated, less carnal, and more noble. It underlies the idea that the body is a temple to be protected from disgusting activities and contamination.

Fig. 6. The foundational concepts of morality.
Adapted from Moral Foundations Theory. https://moralfoundations.org/

Using Moral Foundations Theory, the schism between American liberals and conservatives can be explained as a difference in the emphasis and priorities placed on these building blocks. Liberals rely heavily on morality constructed around care/harm primarily and fairness/cheating secondarily. Conservatives, on the other hand, employ all six foundations and thus are more concerned about loyalty/betrayal, authority/subversion, and sanctity/degradation.

As you meet with your colleagues and talk with them about your project, you may begin to detect foundational differences as reflected in attitudes around:

– How much responsibility your organization should take to reduce harm and destruction in the system

– Whether people who engage in socially undesirable behavior like drug abuse, deserve assistance or disdain

– How much favor one should offer to system outsiders versus insiders

– Whether it is okay to disobey or work around a manager's wishes or to disregard traditions that have been established in your organization or industry

– What one should do in the face of oppression

Once you have identified a colleague's moral drivers, take time to consider how you might frame your project idea in terms of the moral foundations important to that person. The mistake people often make is arguing for a policy using their moral drivers while an argument using the listener's moral drivers would be more effective.

CLAUDIA LORENZO ON
RE-FRAMING THIRST AT COCA-COLA

Claudia Lorenzo was given the mandate at Coca-Cola Brazil to grow the brand and increase penetration in the lower-middle class market. She could have done the usual market-driven research and marketing strategy and invested millions in communication campaigns, but she believed the company needed to look deeper into the reality of families in poor communities in Brazil and understand their true needs and priorities.

With a multidisciplinary team, including an anthropologist and several social entrepreneurs, she spent months visiting low-income communities. A comment from a teenager living in one of the city's shantytowns stayed with her: "We don't have thirst for Coca-Cola; we have thirst for opportunities to grow and make money."

The teenager invited Claudia to reframe her challenge and approach. Claudia realized that Coca-Cola could support the dreams of Brazilian youth in meaningful ways—ways that would help them thrive psychologically and financially, while creating brand loyalty and market penetration as a by-product.

Investing the marketing budget in a program called Coletivo, she aimed to serve young people aged 16 to 25, connecting them to professional development workshops and income generation opportunities. Under Coletivo, youth undertake practical social change projects in their communities, thus acquiring skills in marketing, sales, communication, and event management. At the end of the course, the youth are connected to job opportunities, ongoing studies, and a network of more than 250 employers across the country.

ENERGY BAR

Since the beginning of the program, Coletivo has served more than 219,000 youth in 75 Brazilian communities. Sixty thousand people have been able to access the job market as a result of the program. When comparing Coca-Cola's business results in the communities where Coletivo is present to those where it is not, the program has seen higher growth in sales and brand loyalty.

Over the years, Claudia had the capacity to engage C-suite leaders, as well as the managers of the bottling companies on why this type of investment made sense. She was able to engage everyone by bringing business results attached to social results and this evidence has led to a big shift inside Coca-Cola Brazil towards shared-value opportunities.

Deep Listening

Identifying the existing narratives and moral foundations or worldviews of your audience will require mastering the art of deep listening. Listening is also a core competency for other intrapreneurial ventures like systems mapping, understanding customers and markets, and peer coaching.

Listening is a skill ancient pathfinders would have mastered to tune into nature's cues to guide their journeys. In today's work environments, we are so overloaded with meetings, information, and the pressure to perform that many of us have lost this capacity to really tune in to what is going on around us.

So, what is deep listening?

Deep listening involves listening in a generous, empathic, receptive, and trusting space, with no judgment of what is being said. It is an ongoing practice of suspending self-oriented, reactive thinking and opening one's awareness to what is emerging out of a conversation.

In general, we practice this type of listening when we are in a relaxed, trusted environment with people we care about or when we are traveling in a new place where our full curiosity and openness to learn are activated. Most of the time, in our day-to-day environments, we act as reactive listeners. We are unable to separate our own needs and interests from those of others. Everything that we hear triggers our automatic judgment: "How is this going to affect me?" or "What can I say next to get things my way?"

Using Discerning Questions

When we listen deeply with the goal of understanding, we move into a mode of "discernment" and out of the mode of "judgment." Discernment is about understanding the facts and dynamics of another person's reality, while judgment is about measuring another person against a standard you hold. Even when we pretend not to judge someone negatively, we often unconsciously express our judgement through body language. When the judgement is negative, we may cross our arms, purse our lips, and avoid eye contact.

If you want people who are blocking your intrapreneurial path to move out of the way, you first need to understand their objections. Good discerning questions acknowledge that you do not have all the answers or understand the full context of a person's viewpoint. Discerning questions look like the following:

– "What experiences in your career have led you to believe ___?"

– "That's one option. Here are my concerns with it.
What do you think I am missing?"

– "How do you see your counter-proposal working?"

– "What questions do you have about your hunch/philosophy/ approach? Do you have any doubts? Here are my doubts about my own ideas."

– "What do you make of the criticism that is often made of your idea?"

– "You said ___ and you said ___. I'm confused as to how the two can both be true. How do you see it?"

– "I'm getting the sense that you believe ___. In your experience is that always true, and if not, where isn't it? What would you do about those cases?"

–"You've said: ___. That's not quite how I see it and I'd love to hear more about how you see it. Can you tell me more?"

– "I didn't follow when you said ____. Please help me understand."

Note that in the areas where we left blank spaces, it is wise to repeat your dialogue partner's words verbatim. Most of us are tempted to "interpret" their words and repeat them with a moral judgement. For instance, here are two ways a conversation with your boss might go:

Version One
Boss: "Your idea isn't worth pursuing because our customers don't care about the environment. They care about price."

You: "You're a climate change denier but a lot of people are ready to take action."

Version Two
Boss: "Your idea isn't worth pursuing because our customers don't care about the environment. They care about price."

You: "A moment ago you said our customers 'care about price.' That's certainly true, but they may care about the environment too. Can we run a survey to test their interest?"

The response in Version One interprets the boss's statement as a sign of "climate denial," a term that the boss may see as a moral negative judgement that triggers defensiveness. Version Two's response is a neutral restatement of your boss's position and doesn't seek to change it, but to find a way to work with where your boss is right now. In our experience, Version Two is more likely to advance your project more quickly.

We invite you to practice these types of questions in meetings, and observe how a posture of discernment shifts the dynamics toward a more open conversation.

When we are at our more usual level of listening, we miss the opportunity to access valuable information. Either we are "downloading" (just reconfirming and revising our pre-formed opinions), or in "debate mode" (trying to see how to make our point to convince the other person). We are attending to the specific words rather than listening for what is being said "between the lines." Deep listening is going beyond the words to understand where the other person is coming from and what need or interest is motivating their speech.

A great tool for practicing deep listening is repeating back what you think you are hearing and gently seeking clarification from your counterpart. This allows the other person to feel truly heard and valued and shows your interest in going deeper.

Another key aspect to practicing deep listening is your self-awareness about what sensitivities you have that the other person may react to. Before going into a meeting, it is important to take some time to recognize the biases you hold or what the other person represents to you. This way, you are prepared to not react or let your biases take hold of you during the conversation.

As intrapreneurs, the more we practice deep listening, the more we will find that engaging stakeholders requires less effort and we will uncover opportunities and partnerships previously hidden to us.

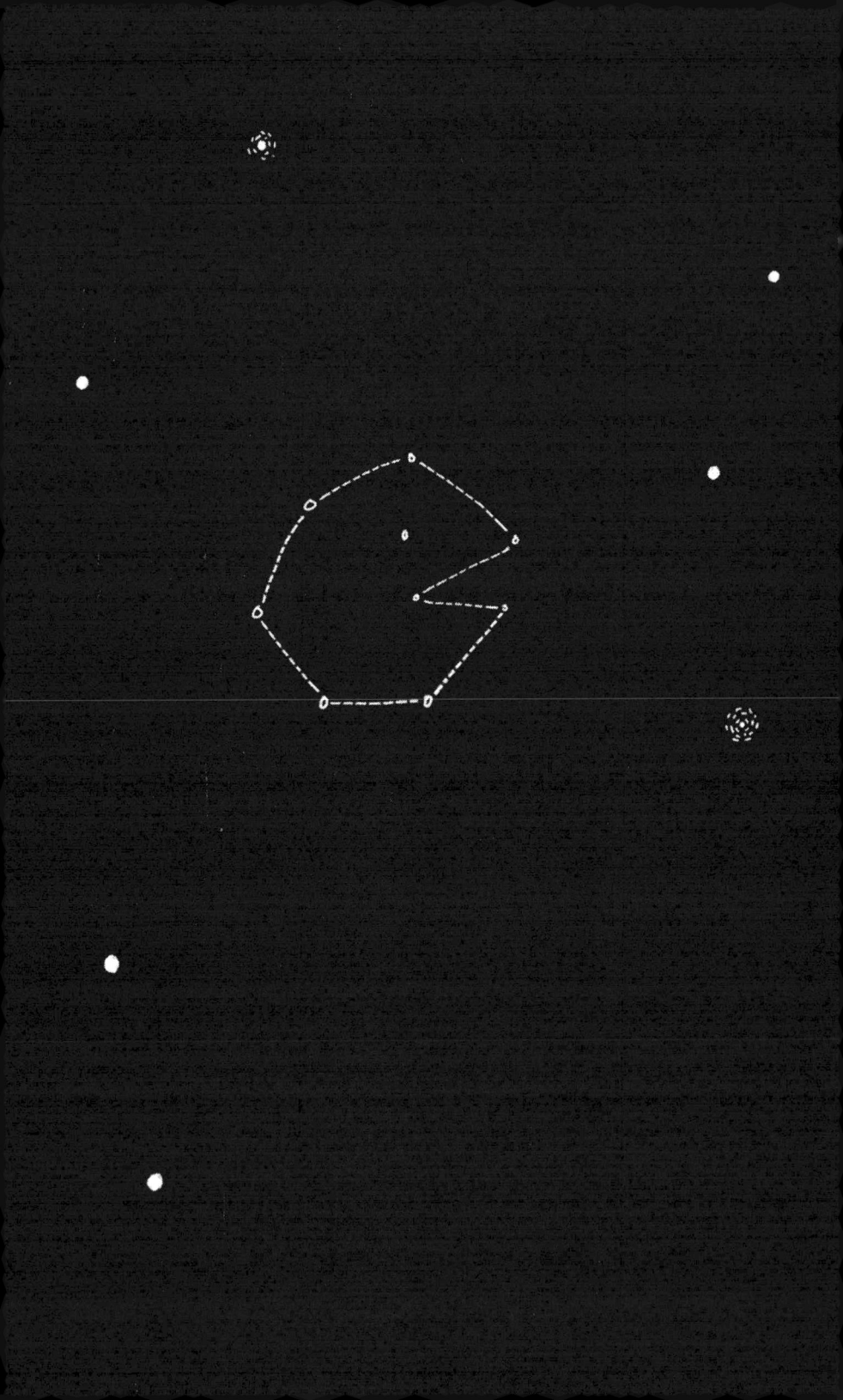

"If we try to listen we find it extraordinarily difficult, because we are always projecting our opinions and ideas, our prejudices, our background, our inclinations, our impulses; when they dominate we hardly listen to what is being said. In that state there is no value at all.

One listens and therefore learns, only in a state of attention, a state of silence in which this whole background is in abeyance, is quiet; then, it seems to me, it is possible to communicate."

J. KRISHNAMURTI, "1ST PUBLIC TALK" (SPEECH, SAANEN, SWITZERLAND, JULY 9, 1967), TALK AND DIALOGUES

Stakeholder Mapping & Recruiting Co-Travelers

If you've done a good job crafting your counter-narrative, you'll recruit co-travelers for the journey.

In *Friend of a Friend: Understanding the Hidden Networks That Can Transform Your Life and Your Career*, David Burkus surveyed the social science research on the power of networks and concluded that, "You're the average of all the people who surround you." The people you choose to hang out with have a statistically significant influence on everything from your physical health to your mental well-being.[36]

The moral? Choose your friends and allies well.

Almost by definition, if you're working in a large organization, you occupy a specific niche and you may have a very specialized and narrow skill set. Because intrapreneurial startups require a wide range of skills, you will need co-travelers from sales and marketing, data analysis, communication, strategic planning, and process planning, etc. You will also need co-travelers or champions higher up the organizational food chain to provide "air cover"—permission, mentoring, and resourcing.

If you have taken the time to consult with a wide array of stakeholders in Chapter Two's goal setting phase, you likely already have a very good idea of who might complement your skill set and want to join the expedition. What gifts do they offer? Who is missing from your team?

Stakeholder mapping can help you identify and categorize your stakeholders. You can plot the relevant stakeholders in a simple 2x2 matrix defined by the actor's level of power (as demonstrated in the diagram opposite), and their level of interest in your project. If you're unsure about their interest level, ask colleagues who know them, set up one-on-one interviews where possible, or at the very least try gauging their interest by examining their LinkedIn profiles or Googling them. You would be amazed at how many clues these sources will offer.

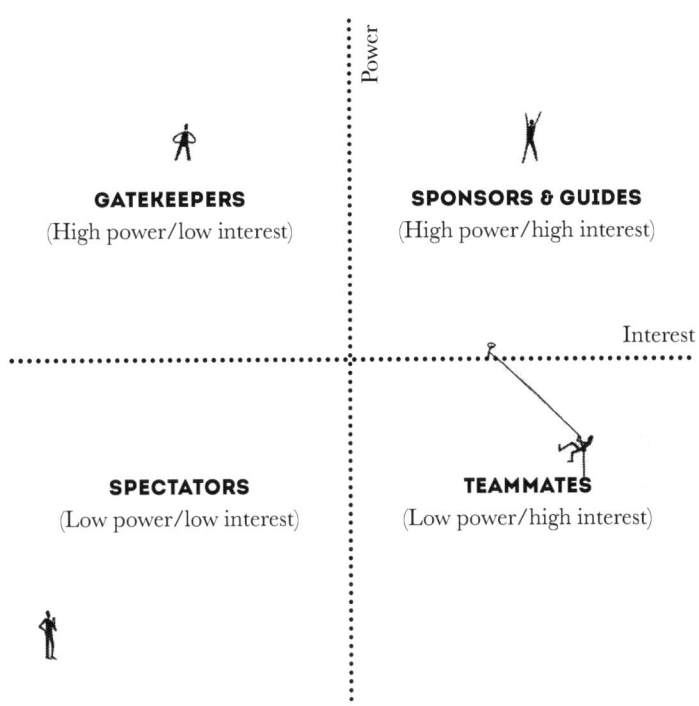

Fig. 7. Stakeholder mapping can help you identify and categorize co-travelers by their levels of power and interest.

Gatekeepers (High power/low interest): Try to increase this group's interest around your project. Engage and consult them strategically.

Sponsors & Guides (High power/high interest): Rally this group around your project. Focus your advocacy on this group and try to involve them in the governance of your project. Engage and consult them regularly.

Spectators (Low power/low interest): Try to increase this group's interest around your project. Engage and consult them where possible.

Teammates (Low power/high interest): Rally this group around your project and work most closely with them. They are likely to be the people who see what you see and want new policies, practices, and resourcing changes.

This initial mapping will indicate different strategies for each quadrant. You'll want to keep Sponsors and Guides closely involved and your Teammates closest to the work. You should ensure you keep Gatekeepers on side and consult and engage with them to help increase their interest over time. In the short-term, however, make sure you meet their needs and don't give them any reasons to close doors. Spectators are a lower priority for engagement, but consider low-touch ways to keep them apprised of progress to help increase their support over time.

One thing to be aware of in identifying co-travelers at your office is hidden influencers who may or may not show up as powerful in terms of their titles, but who are clearly powerful in terms of how they influence what happens and how people think about an issue. The following questions from the School for Social Entrepreneurs Canada's program on intrapreneurship can help you identify these people (see opposite).

Once you've got your initial co-traveler map, develop strategies for engaging each of the players and cultivating more support. Set up meetings to learn:

— What drives them?

— Are they in it for reward and recognition?

— Do they get satisfaction from being part of a team?

— Are they a protector of the brand?

— Do they enjoy exploring new terrain?

— Do they have other pressures of which you may not be aware? How can you find out?

Building a diverse coalition around your idea will increase the likelihood that it will garner support across the organization, be executed faithfully, and will survive even when you're gone.

Identifying Hidden Influencers at Work

Who gets invited to most or all meetings?

Whose jokes are always laughed at, even when not funny?

Who decides what is discussed in team meetings versus behind closed doors?

Who does the boss listen to?

Who gets the most information because people share it with them?

Who decides compensation?

Who gets non-monetary perks?

When people go out after work, who always gets invited?

Who determines who gets to talk to the boss?

Who determines the speed at which things get done?

Who sabotages plans?

Who is the "office clown?"

Who does everyone adore?

We also recommend that you take time to find out what good work is already happening outside your organization so that you don't unwittingly crowd out or compete with good projects already underway. Often, community-based social entrepreneurs have great ideas, but enjoy very few resources or recognition from the outside. Partnering with grassroots innovators can help ideas that are developed by affected communities and allow them to scale. We have heard woeful stories of grassroots leaders who say they worked for years on an initiative only to have someone with a bigger budget and brand take their ideas and claim credit.

MIKI STRICKER-TALBOT ON FINDING CO-TRAVELERS

Miki is a League Fellow and government intrapreneur at the City of Edmonton in Canada. By 2016, she had witnessed many talented colleagues flee the public service in frustration. Along with her colleague Barb Ursuliak, she decided to start a peer safety net group. When deciding what to call the peer group, Barb and Miki joked that their fellow municipal government intrapreneurs were mythical unicorns who found themselves so far out in front, they'd hit the wall with their horns. The United Network of Innovative Change-agents Organizing to Realize New Strategies (U.N.I.C.O.R.N.S.) launched one spring morning with an invitation to 14 changemakers. By the end of the day, the invitation list had doubled to 29. The U.N.I.C.O.R.N.S. took off. By 2019, the numbers had hit 171. Today, in public service pockets across the country and around the world, change agents have started to form their own U.N.I.C.O.R.N.S.-inspired groups within government. Because of the efforts of people like Miki and Barb, these pathfinders no longer need to travel alone.

Leveraging the Talents of Your Team

It is good to know how to harness the strengths of your team members. Who has a talent for organization or skill in garnering resources? If one member of the group is adept at spotting trends and another has skills in converting ideas into action, that knowledge is useful in assigning tasks in a way that will boost the chances of success. In short, it's critical to recruit a large contingent of co-travelers to take the journey with you, because people survive better in numbers. They organize to help one another, to carry out necessary tasks, and to keep each other motivated and energized.

Here are the co-travelers that successful intrapreneurial teams include:

The intrapreneur:
The project catalyst,
which is probably you.

The fast follower:
The person who can
convert ideas
into action.

The scribe:
The person who
documents the process
of innovation.

**The front-line
innovator:** The frugal
problem solver who can
make more with less.

The shaman:
The person who builds
team capacity and
facilitates interactions.

The scanner:
The trend spotter
who identifies new
opportunities
and threats.

The stabilizer:
The shepherd of
tradition who ensures
that innovation is built on
the foundation of what
has worked in the past.

The net-weaver:
The connector and
bridge builder who can
serve as an ambassador
for your project.

The disruptor:
The person who has
new ideas for the
team to try.

The fairy godmother:
The wise elder who
can run interference
and be your protective
champion when things
get tough.

Some intrapreneurs are especially lucky to work for "shamans," or other intrapreneurs who can provide political cover for a project. One such intrapreneurial supervisor in the League anonymously shared how he has tried to create and nurture a culture that prioritizes intrapreneurship:

> "Intrapreneurial thinking is a documented principle of our team. In postings for positions, the word 'intrapreneurship' is advertised. I ask interview questions about intrapreneurship. Once I have the right people, I work to create a safe space that allows them to thrive. We have blue sky sessions where we talk through strategies and work using the toolkits provided by the League and others. I practice authenticity and vulnerability as a leader, and I encourage the team to do the same … but this has come at a significant price. I've been told I need to stop hiring 'deliberately challenging women' by a boss. I'm told I will not be promoted because I don't punish my team for mistakes (we reward risk and failure, rather than punish it). I have been told I will never advance my career at my organization because of this. However, I fundamentally believe it's the right thing to do. Government needs intrapreneurs."

In many teams, one or several people can play multiple roles; ideally, all roles are represented, but you should prioritize the intrapreneur and the fairy godmother. These two are essential for making it through.

If you're not lucky enough to work for a shaman, think about how you can foster an intrapreneurial environment for those around you.

Stoking Your Team's Fire and Keeping It Burning

The counter-narrative you've offered or created with your team will ignite a fire. How do you keep it burning?

Few intrapreneurial teams will literally burn something, but they all will need a metaphorical fire to sustain their spirits.

Fire is elemental. Human mastery of the burning process has offered us light, warmth, clean water, and cooked food for hundreds of thousands of years. Making fire requires three ingredients: oxygen, heat, and fuel.

Oxygen is abundant in the air, and like oxygen, the words and stories your team creates and shares will serve as a key ingredient in keeping the intrapreneurial flame alive. Be sure you're leading with the compelling new story that you developed earlier. Remind yourself frequently why you started your intrapreneurial project in the first place.

Heat, the second ingredient for a fire, needs to come from a source of ignition. When it comes to actual fires, ignition can come either from friction (e.g., rubbing two sticks together) or concentrating heat (e.g., using a magnifying glass to focus the sun's rays.) If your organization is plagued by complaints that your employer has lost its way or that it has come under unwelcome media attention due to scandals and bad behavior, irritating frictions offer the perfect opportunity to strike a team fire that fuels your quest.

Alternatively, your team may be motivated by passion for a great organization that they feel could be magnified with some positive changes. For instance, if you're working at an NGO and received an industry award, your government has recently changed political administration, or your company has become a media darling, you can use these developments as an opportunity to form an intrapreneurial team to capitalize on optimism and ensure that your employer continues to deserve this public vote of confidence.

Whatever the source of the heat, the fire of team spirit won't get going without fuel to feed and sustain it. Where does the fuel come from? The first fuel that the fledgling fire needs to consume is a quick project win, a clump of metaphorical tinder. These quick wins can come in the form of convening a group and finding common purpose. Tinder burns out quickly, but can ignite the second fuel called kindling, the source of embers. Create opportunities for team members to contribute something meaningful to the project immediately after they meet and agree to work together. A sense of forward momentum will ensure that this kindling burns hot enough to light the third fuel, firewood. Firewood represents well-established intrapreneurial initiatives that have traction in the organization and are really starting to create change within the culture. Note that firewood can burn indefinitely as long as more firewood is added. According to many Cherokee people, a sacred fire exists today that has long-sustained their community, burning continuously for over a thousand years.

Keep the Fire Burning

Everyone working on an intrapreneurial project should know and be honest about the strengths and weaknesses of those in their party. Some people need more time to rest. Some cannot venture as far or fast as others.

Good leaders nurture the emotional health of their teammates by taking different needs into account and celebrating the wins collectively when the project hits a milestone. They also tend to the team's fire when it is cast into difficult situations. One simple way to gauge team members' energy is to check in before meetings by asking people to share how they are feeling. This allows the team to focus attention where it may be most needed and ensure no one gets left behind.

As an intrapreneur, you'll want to keep a close eye on the energy source for your fire. How can you direct frustration and sadness about politics and the environment toward positive action? How can you transform hope into a source of warmth and protection in a cold world? Just as uncontrolled fire can rage and burn down the forest, you must direct your team's fire carefully and ensure that it is contained safely. If you notice bitterness and resentment beginning to fuel the team spirit, gently encourage the team to draw its fire from "cleaner" sources of energy, like solidarity, compassion, and a desire to serve.

Planning for Succession

Your venture needs to be self-sustaining beyond any one leader. Once you prove a new model, how can you institutionalize the idea? Plan for succession early on, exploring potential internal and external partners who can pick up if and when you move on and can't keep stoking the fire. Your leadership team will be far more robust as a result.

You'll need to identify key influencers within your organization and get them on your side. A champion or leader can offer you protection, but be careful not to become anyone's pet project. Some intrapreneurs who are overly aligned with a particular CEO or senior manager struggle to find support when their sponsor gets promoted, transferred, or fired. Try to integrate the project into the core priorities of the organization so that it is not dependent on transient personnel.

In addition, ask your team's scribe to document your project along the way. If for some reason, you have to abandon the excursion, a future organizational pathfinder can pick up where you left off. A quest that might be unachievable today could be achievable tomorrow.

For instance, Carl Muñana developed a blueprint for building out an impact investing practice while he was at JP Morgan in Mexico in 1998. His venture was unfortunately killed off by factors related to a Russian financial crisis, but many years later his blueprint was picked up again by another intrapreneur, Henry Gonzalez, at Morgan Stanley. The result was the company's Social Finance Group that extends capital and impact investment funds to low-income and excluded communities. Many times, intrapreneurial ventures are born before their time.

How does my team move toward the unknown?
What can I learn from those who went before?
How will we measure impact?
How will we keep track of our progress
and monitor travel conditions?

4

Journeying Into the Unknown

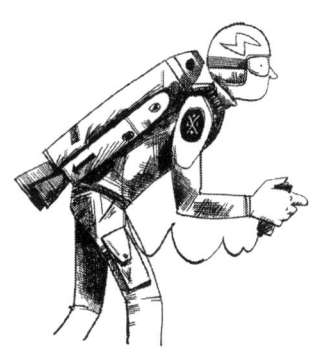

Your team has done all the planning and preparation. Now it's time to get a move on. The initial steps are likely to feel exciting and wonderful. But then someone will trip and sprain an ankle, or the group will get totally turned around. At some point, you'll probably start to worry that you've made a mistake in proposing this adventure.

Understand that setbacks and disorientation are perfectly normal and to be expected when out exploring the wilderness. The key to making your way through unknown terrain is to anticipate and plan, and to maintain a healthy attitude—getting lost can be half the fun.

If you're navigating in low-visibility conditions, you'll need to determine your present position and identify the intended destination and direction of travel (the purpose of Chapters One and Two). In this chapter, we offer a set of concepts that will help you make tactical decisions about getting a move on and covering the distance to your destination.

Assessing Current Travel Conditions

Before setting out, you'll need to consider the current travel conditions.

How's the Weather?

If your organization is in the middle of a crisis, it may welcome big intrapreneurial ideas that address the root cause of the crisis or it may make the organization extraordinarily risk averse for fear of attracting even more negative attention. The point is to assess whether there's more openness to experimentation due to a change in the political winds. If there is, you may be able to attempt a risky intrapreneurial voyage that wouldn't be possible under normal conditions.

As historian Mauricio Obregón explains:

> "If, like Columbus, one is going to sail across an ocean toward a great continent, one goes with the prevailing wind, as Columbus did; but if like the Polynesians, one is going to sail out into an apparently limitless ocean in search of an island that may or may not be there, it is wiser to wait for one of those days when the wind blows contrary to its prevailing direction. Then, if the island does not turn up, instead of being blown away indefinitely, one can simply wait for the prevailing wind to return, and can sail home to try again another day."[37]

Is the Timing Right to Travel?

Certain times or milestones within a company can cause an employer to pause and reflect on its organizational identity or decide it's time to "reinvigorate" the organization with fresh ideas. This can be an opportunity for you to present your project. Or perhaps there is newfound openness to introducing purpose into the workplace? SK Group, one of the four largest conglomerates in Korea, recently changed the way it evaluates employees. It now assesses them equally on how much economic and social value they create. Jeongtae Kim, a League Catalyst based in Seoul, says this change has created dramatic growth of corporate social intrapreneurs inside SK. Catalina Garcia Gomez, an intrapreneur and Global Director of Corporate Affairs at drink and brewing company AB InBev had dreamed of using the brewing process to make hand sanitizer for communities with poor access to sanitation. Once the COVID-19 pandemic hit, the timing was perfect and she was able to transform this idea into reality and support frontline workers in the hardest hit areas.[38]

Should You Travel in Stealth?

Some groups work in secret or well below the active attention of their colleagues. For instance, the "calling janitors" mentioned in Chapter One added secret tasks of hospital diplomacy that made their jobs more meaningful, such as consoling visibly upset patients and hosting visiting families by walking visitors to the parking lot and offering them water.[39] For the most part, these tasks were done out of view of supervisors who might consider these positive behaviors as an unwelcome challenge to current, accepted practice. Define whether your intrapreneurial team is able to move in full view of your colleagues or if it needs to operate under the cover of darkness until you've collected the evidence you need to garner buy-in.

How Much Time Should You Budget?

To calculate the distance you and your travel companions will need for the journey, first measure the distance between the start and end points on your mental map. If you did your homework in Chapter One, you'll have a good sense of where you are now and where you want to go. Now, you'll need to guesstimate travel time, a tricky thing to do.

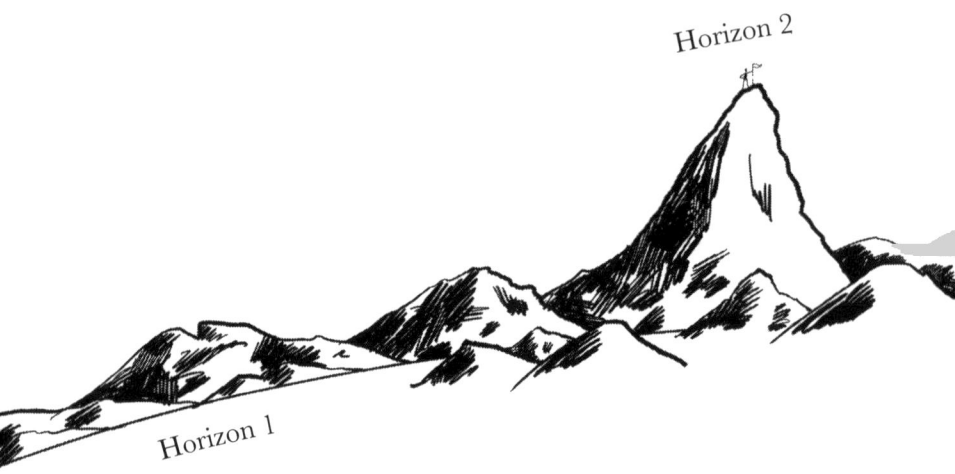

Horizon 2

Horizon 1

A common framework for understanding innovation distance is the Three Horizons model mentioned in Chapter One. In this model—equally applicable to businesses, governments, and NGOs—innovation is understood to happen in one of three horizons:

- Horizon one ideas incrementally improve an organization's existing business or operating model and core capabilities in the short-term.

- Horizon two ideas extend the business or operating model and core capabilities to an adjacent area (e.g., new programs, clients, customers, markets, or targets).

- Horizon three ideas transform a business or operating model and core capabilities to take advantage of or respond to disruption in the wider system.

Traditionally, the rule of thumb is that horizon one ideas can be implemented in three to 12 months, while horizon two extensions are completed in 24 to 36 months and horizon three transformations require 36 to 72 months. However, as Steve Blank argues in the article "McKinsey's Three Horizons Model Defined Innovation for Years. Here's Why It No Longer Applies," disruption is so much easier to achieve now given the cheap and easy access to technology like smartphones and app creation.[40] As such, horizon three innovations can occur in the same timeframe as horizon one ideas. That said, taking on deeply entrenched systems usually requires years to see meaningful

impact. Professor Muhammad Yunus set up Grameen Bank in 1983, but it wasn't until over a decade later that microfinance entered the mainstream. He won the Nobel Peace Prize in 2006, 23 years later.

Being able to estimate how long an intrapreneurial project might take is genuinely difficult, and the answer will depend on your organization's appetite for disruption. The answer will also depend on whether you're creating something from scratch or improvising with whatever is already at hand, "bricolage" style. You'll also need to take into account your travel pace and that of your companions and the organization at large. If you're traveling in a wide open field with natural intrapreneurs who are trusted, you may cover the distance rapidly; if you're in a highly bureaucratic jungle with first-time innovators, you may need to budget for longer travel time.

Whether you're journeying toward horizon two or horizon three, give your best guess of a timeframe for your project and then add 50 percent or more. You'll go in with more realistic expectations, worry less about the slow pace of change, and better manage precious resources like time and money.

Keep Asking Questions

Although you may have defined a guiding "higher order" question for your quest, you should continue to use questions to steer you as you move through the project terrain. Some authors like Hal Gregerson argue that innovation is really just about asking a series of good questions that build on one another.

We at the League believe in the power of questions so much that our in-person gatherings often center on question-asking groups called "Case Clinics." Case Clinics are inspired by the methodology known as action learning (AL), a problem-solving approach pioneered by Reg Revans in the 1940s. AL is recognized as an unusually simple, but powerful method of widening participants' perspectives through powerful, open-ended questions. Large corporations, governmental agencies, and non-profits including Sony, Anglo American Mining, GE, Deutsche Bank, and the UN Environment Programme have all used AL for breakthrough innovation.

In the League's Case Clinics, teams of four to six people engage in a collaborative problem-solving process. Together they reflect on real-time workplace or project issues facing a particular intrapreneur. Through skillful questions that follow an AL format and philosophy of inquiry, the Case Clinic participants help the intrapreneur explore possible solutions, and plan for action. Case Clinics are particularly valuable in helping League members develop greater awareness of how their behaviors, attitudes, and assumptions affect their decision-making and intrapreneurial plan.

Tim Mahlberg of the League of Intrapreneurs Australia says:

"I experienced my first League Case Clinic where we split into small circles to support one person in finding their intrapreneurial path in their organization and profession. I was struck by the compassion, consideration, and encouragement that left the case sharer with tangible next steps, plenty of food for thought, and importantly, ongoing access to expertise and support as needed."

If you're unable to join a League Case Clinic, you can learn how to formulate powerful, open-ended questions through online resources. "The Art of Powerful Questions" by Eric E. Vogt, Juanita Brown, and David Isaacs offers a framework for understanding what makes a question powerful (specifically construction, underlying assumptions, and scope). Also a simple Google search on "powerful questions" will point you toward myriad coaching websites with lists of questions you can pose to yourself and your team.

The League employs a "question storming" exercise similar to a brainstorming session that is particularly valuable when intrapreneurs feel stuck. The format helps avoid groupthink and invites participants to contribute not answers, but open-ended, powerful questions. One person poses a problem in the form of a question and then others reflect on the topic and think of questions, which are jotted down quickly on individual sticky notes. This stage usually lasts a few minutes or up to 20 minutes, with the aim of producing as many questions as possible.

Participants then review the questions and group them together by theme. For each thematic group, the questions are assessed for their construction, underlying assumptions, and scope, then refined and wordsmithed until a powerful synthesized question emerges. The objective is to look for questions that help reframe the problem or reexamine the problem-holder's approach. We advise repeating the exercise a few times until useful insights emerge.

Covering the Distance with Prototyping & Experimenting

If you're asking yourself questions, you'll be looking for answers. Some of us will be in a greater hurry to find them.

If you took the League Intrapreneur Quotient™ assessment and your score was in the "natural intrapreneur" range, this is both good and bad news. It's great that you have lots of intrapreneurial energy and drive. The challenge will be that you might see the destination far off in the distance and not think twice about speeding off like a cheetah. While you may, at times, choose to go ahead of the group and return, it is important to set a pace for the trip that takes into account the slowest participants.

Justin DeKoszmovszky, a natural intrapreneur and League Catalyst, shared his story of intrapreneurial woe when he got too far ahead of others at SC Johnson, a global household cleaning supplies and chemical company:

> "When I worked at SC Johnson, I created a circular product-as-a-service model in low-income Nairobi communities. We iterated our way into it, but the business model was so different from the company's linear consumer good distributor-retailer model that the local and global leadership didn't know how to help us scale. The business, Community Cleaning Services, was spun out as a city-scale social enterprise, but struggled and has shrunk to only operating in one community. I often wonder what we might have been able to achieve with more service or franchise expertise in the parent company."

One of the best ways to build intrapreneurial capacity in your co-travelers and to build confidence is to start finding answers with a few rapid rounds of prototyping and experimenting and using the results of those trial runs as evidence that the organization needs to build up greater expertise in areas of weakness. You should treat your prototype like a hypothesis that you are trying to validate or invalidate. By setting up small experiments to test your ideas, you can work around the traditionally onerous vetting that occurs in big bureaucracies for full-scale projects.

Ian Howatt's team in the City of Edmonton in Canada has found that prototyping actually reduces overall risk: "We try quickly [with prototypes that use] minimal resources, test, and iterate with an enhanced version. In this way, we're reducing the risk of launching a large systems change that ultimately fails." Ian's team pushed to integrate "strategic foresight" approaches into the city's planning processes. He and his teammates were unable to gain approval for a sweeping new approach, but they were successful in prototyping foresight in small projects with key leaders that can become champions for the team down the road.

Prototyping and Testing Your Idea

Prototyping is just a fancy word for visualizing and mocking up your idea to quickly get feedback and insight. There are four dimensions for prototyping:

1. Understanding:

How can we learn more about the needs of our users?

2. Inspiring:

How can we help people to see what is possible?

3. Involving:

How can we enroll and involve others in problem solving?

4. Validating:

How can we learn and fail fast (and cheaply)?

You don't have to be a designer to be great at prototyping. Remember those arts and crafts you did as a child? Channel this playful hands-on energy to make your prototypes. Simple tools like pens, cardboard, and glue sticks can be applied to great effect in a mockup of an experience or product. Test your skills in low-risk environments to build up confidence. Prototyping is also a process to help you understand the problem better. James Dyson famously made thousands of prototypes before producing his first bagless vacuum cleaner.

You can involve a large group in a prototype process by running a hackathon wherein the group comes up with workable ideas during a time-limited sprint (often a one- or two-day process). You'll likely surprise yourselves. Google Ventures, for example, regularly does a product design sprint where it works with startups over a short period of time (five days) to accelerate and unstick projects. They've noticed that often the best work comes out in short bursts and under time constraints.

Another approach to getting a move on is to take a scientific approach. Eric Ries in *The Lean Startup* talks about "minimum viable products" (MVPs) where you start with what you need to learn, build only what you need in order to gain that knowledge, and then run an experiment to get that measurement. Experimentation will help you to hone in on a clear and simple solution. For ventures delivering impact, this logic is essential. Many products suffer when they are bundled with too many features, a result of not clearly understanding the core need they're addressing. Get out into the field and really understand what a community needs and then design a feature that has a clear line of sight back to those needs.

A real-world example of an MVP can be found at Buffer, the social media management company. Founder Joel Gascoigne zeroed in on an idea to take the "scheduling feature of many Twitter clients and apps and make that single feature awesome."[41] Without a product, Buffer launched a two-page website that promoted a software that would publish users' tweets at scheduled times. Gascoigne used the site to gauge how many people would be interested in using the product and also if they would pay for it. Based on that feedback, which validated the idea and pricing, Gascoigne developed the actual software and has grown the product, adding new features and integrations with other social media platforms.

Prototypes, hackathons, and experiments are all forms of rapid iteration. They will help your team get moving, secure some quick wins, learn more about the problem, and get feedback. For practical tips on prototyping, check out IDEO's Design Kit and Stanford's d.school.

Innovation Launchpads

Innovation rarely occurs in the form of a lone genius moment. More often, innovation is prompted by inspiration from other innovators. That's why we've created this framework of innovation thought-starters to serve as jumping off points to help you find your world-changing idea.

PURPOSEFUL BRANDS & MOVEMENTS

Intrapreneurs are harnessing the power of brands and social movements to create impact. Ask yourself: "How might we connect to intrinsic values, not just 'green' propositions?"

Inspiring examples: Patagonia's "Don't Buy this Jacket" advertising campaign launched on the so-called "Black Friday" shopping holiday in the United States in an attempt to shift people away from mindless consumption.

Time's Up is a collaborative initiative started by 300 leading women in Hollywood on the back of the popular #MeToo movement, advancing practical actions to create safe, equitable workplaces for women.

THE POWER OF WE

Intrapreneurs are creating platforms that democratize access and shift the balance of power. Ask yourself: "How might we decentralize decision-making and create platforms for citizen power?"

Inspiring examples: Paris has set up a participatory budgeting scheme, "Madame Mayor, I have an idea," which is allocating €500 million to projects proposed by citizens between 2014 and 2020.

Olio is a food sharing platform designed to eliminate food waste by enabling people with leftover food to share it with their neighbors using a simple mobile app.

HACKING ASSETS

Intrapreneurs are applying the core competencies and assets of their organizations to solve wicked challenges. Ask yourself: "How might we better leverage our existing assets to enable impactful collaborations?"

Inspiring examples: Project Last Mile is a collaboration between The Coca-Cola Company, The Global Fund, USAID, and The Bill & Melinda Gates Foundation. The project harnesses Coca-Cola's cold supply chain and marketing expertise to help more efficiently deliver critical vaccines, medicines, and medical supplies in hard-to-reach markets.

AXA, a global insurance company, is applying insurance tools to help address economic development. Insurance helps people to take more calculated risks, thereby enabling low-income families to invest in things like farm equipment and education that help them to create more sustainable livelihoods.

THINK OPEN

Intrapreneurs are committed to harnessing the power of data and transparency to shift systems. Ask yourself: "How might we share data and increase transparency?"

Inspiring examples: Ushahidi is a crowd-sourcing platform that enables citizens to upload data so that areas of need—from political violence to natural disasters—are easier to spot and so that those who can provide assistance can more easily reach them.

Levi's spent nine years perfecting its process to reduce water use by 96 percent from the manufacture of its denim products. It now offers that insight open source.

RADICAL COLLABORATION

Intrapreneurs are on a constant quest to find the right partners to deliver. Ask yourself: "How might we build trusted relationships with unlikely allies?"

Inspiring examples: Toyota and Suzuki's "Tie-up" is an unlikely partnership between fierce competitors to advance hybrid and electric vehicle technology that "will help give us the competitive edge we will need to survive this once-in-a-century period of profound transformation."[42]

Red Cross Australia and Swinburne University are partnering to develop a social connection technology to help people assess the strength of their relationships. This is part of a broader initiative to #beatloneliness, tackling increased loneliness in our communities.

Measuring Distance Traveled:
Impact Measurement Milestones

On a long journey, everyone wants to know how far they've gone and how long until they reach their destination. Survey any parent who travels with kids in the back seat of the car asking, "Are we there yet?"

In the domain of social impact, evaluating a project against performance milestones can be a complex and rigorous undertaking. The process involves collecting and analyzing data around a project's activities and outcomes against measures of effectiveness or process quality. A good project monitoring and evaluation plan can help improve project design and implementation, and also demonstrate societal impact to your organization, the intended beneficiaries, and the general public.

Evaluation typically falls into one of two broad groups: formative and summative. Formative evaluations help determine how best to achieve your goals and/or improve your project offering. They are carried out during program development and implementation. Summative evaluations are designed to tell you how well the program is achieving its goals.

Each type of evaluation requires different tools depending on the nature and stage of the work. For instance, many projects want to estimate how life would have been different had they not been undertaken. This is called estimating the "counterfactual" case, and social innovators who take this question very seriously might conduct a type of evaluation used extensively in medicine known as randomized controlled trials (RCT).

Under an RCT, one group receives a "treatment" like a program, service, or access to a product, while a second group does not. Both groups must start as equally likely or eligible to receive the given treatment, but randomization determines which people actually receive it. The next stage of an RCT compares differences of outcomes between the two groups in order to estimate the impact of the program.

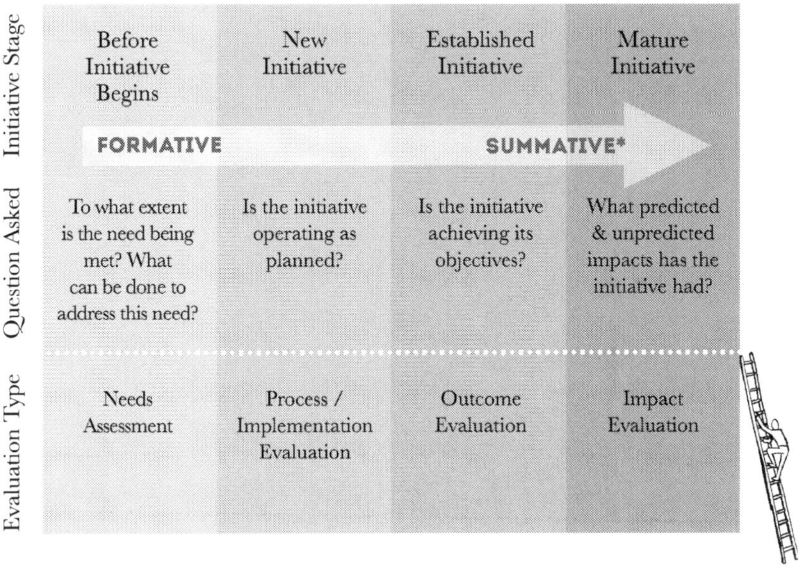

	Before Initiative Begins	New Initiative	Established Initiative	Mature Initiative
Initiative Stage	FORMATIVE		SUMMATIVE*	
Question Asked	To what extent is the need being met? What can be done to address this need?	Is the initiative operating as planned?	Is the initiative achieving its objectives?	What predicted & unpredicted impacts has the initiative had?
Evaluation Type	Needs Assessment	Process / Implementation Evaluation	Outcome Evaluation	Impact Evaluation

Fig. 8. Evaluation framework demonstrates how summative evaluations build on data collected in the earlier stages. From My Environmental Education Evaluation Resource Assistant (MEERA). http://meera.snre.umich.edu/evaluation-what-it-and-why-do-it.

CHAPTER FOUR

Conducting a proper RCT requires a sophisticated evaluation program design, which must be planned in advance. Most social intrapreneurs are not in a position to undertake an evaluation this rigorous, so they usually opt for modest methods like conducting interviews with people who are experts familiar with the beneficiary group. Obviously, this type of evaluation is easier to conduct, though quite a bit less reliable.

The point is that measuring the distance traveled in your project can be a very complex matter or a simple one depending on how robust you need the findings to be. If you want to aim high, we recommend either hiring a monitoring and evaluation consultant in your area, partnering with a local university with impact evaluation capacities, and/or exploring evaluation resources online like BetterEvaluation. There, you will find an introduction to the dozens and dozens of monitoring and evaluation methods, strategies, and processes to determine which one might be right for you. BetterEvaluation's planning tools can help you commission and manage an evaluation, plan an evaluation, check the quality of an ongoing evaluation, amplify the voices of program participants in evaluation, and develop evaluation capacity.

Whatever you decide, we highly recommend planning for monitoring and evaluation at the outset. It is much easier to collect data along the way than to reconstruct it after the fact. This advice is particularly relevant if you will be evaluating changes in behaviors or opinions as these changes can be harder to recall later. By planning ahead of time and gathering baseline data at the start, you position yourself for success and will have an easier time assessing change.

Many intrapreneurs in the League community and beyond use the UN SDGs as a framework for defining impact. The SDGs enumerate a set of 17 objectives to be achieved by 2030 in areas related to poverty, inequality, climate, environmental degradation, prosperity, and peace and justice.[43] All interconnected, they set out a vision that has been informed by a very wide range of stakeholders and that is supported widely by country governments, companies, and civil society.

By no means does your intrapreneurial project need to be tied to the SDGs, but the list of 17 goals is well considered and comes with extensive, accompanying research and sub-objectives that you can use to organize your field research and goal setting.

If the SDGs are not the right framework for your context, consider third-party frameworks set out by your city, industry, or country. All good impact frameworks come with key performance indicators that you can use to measure the distance traveled (and/or your contribution to the goal) as you move through the formative and summative stages of a project.

Fig. 9. The 17 UN SDGs. From the UN.
https://sustainabledevelopment.un.org/sdgs

The advantage of employing a third-party framework is that they will likely have been developed by evaluation experts. As such, they will theoretically be well-considered; they are often free, and they can facilitate apples-to-apples comparisons between your project and others offered by different groups.

The last thing we'll say about measuring the distance traveled is that your yardstick may differ from your colleagues. Colleen McCormick is a government intrapreneur in British Columbia, Canada. She feels that the way intrapreneurs measure success is what sets them apart:

> "How I measure progress and successes in projects I understand is quite different than my colleagues. I have learned over the years that what I care the most about, others care less about as many are results driven, while I'm often behaviour/attitude/mindset focused. I constantly assess the conditions and readiness for transformative change. As I reflect deeper on what I measure, I think about the transformative capacity of initiatives more than other elements of my work. I get excited about changing mindsets. What I am striving to achieve is much different than my peers. My boss laughs at the things I pay attention to in meetings, but those features are the things that matter the most to me. Intrapreneurs focus differently on their efforts and how we measure our impact and track progress."

Recognize that your project may need to have multiple measures that offer something to everyone.

QUESTIONS TO ASK YOURSELF
How will we feed our project out in the wild?
How will we stay resilient?

5

Making Sure You're Equipped

Feeding Your Project

Surviving in the wild is a calories game. Every action we take—even the act of looking for calories—consumes calories. Intrapreneurial projects require human talents, permission, time, and money to sustain themselves. Missing any one of these categories of balanced nutrition will compromise the health of your initiative. Should the project consume more calories than it can acquire, it will lose vigor and collapse when the calories run out.

A growing number of employers are beginning to see the value of intrapreneurship and have started programs to foster intrapreneurial projects (see the Energy Bar on page 142). While this is an encouraging trend, it is still the exception to the rule, and most social intrapreneurs will be operating in environments where they need to scrounge for every project calorie they can find.

Finding food sources for intrapreneurial ventures isn't easy, but training on what to look for in the wild will help you spot them faster. Once acquired, you'll need to convert lean ingredients into a tasty meal that will help your project not only survive, but also thrive.

In the next section, we offer general advice on securing organizational assets for your project, and then we offer advice specific to different types of resources.

Securing Institutional Assets

KEEP YOUR PITCH FAMILIAR BUT ALLURING

Your pitch should be familiar, but not so common that the organization can get what you have to offer elsewhere and easily.

For instance, an insurance industry intrapreneur who prefers to remain nameless wanted permission to work on innovative responses to climate change. Her boss didn't want her to spend time on climate change, but when the intrapreneur presented the work as a way to develop competence in new data analysis techniques through artificial intelligence and blockchain technologies (something her department was looking at already), the project seemed a lot more familiar but also different enough to be alluring.

DON'T ASK TOO SOON

Gifford Pinchot III says the only thing worse than scaring your colleagues with "too big a vision" is asking for money too soon. He writes:

"Ask too soon for too much and there is a good chance that you will get some version of 'No!' Once someone has denied you resources, rationalization sets in: if they refused to provide resources, then your idea must be bad, otherwise they made a bad decision not to support it. The more they say 'no' to it, the worse your idea becomes in their minds."

It's better to ask for time, permission, and human resources first.[44]

DON'T SPOOK YOUR COLLEAGUES

Never seek funds too close to co-workers' money pots, or they may become suspicious and worry you are trying to steal their resources.

Defensiveness will set in and they may rally to kill your project.

ATTRACT ATTENTION WITH A SUCCESSFUL PROTOTYPE

Build your prototype with foraged resources and hold it out as bait for bigger ones. Show how the prototype represents a solution to a significant problem the organization needs solved. Yun Hui Hong of eBay Korea offered the company a chance at a new market:

> "We could have developed a huge product range before launching CarePlus but we didn't because we wanted to start small yet quick. Once we'd done that and gathered feedback from a more diverse group of users, we gradually added more categories and more products to expand the range."

Read more about Yun Hui Hong later in this chapter.

ASK FOR ADVICE

In his song "Feel This Moment," rapper Pitbull declares, "Ask for money, and get advice. Ask for advice, get money twice." Many a Silicon Valley entrepreneur would agree. It is often much easier to ask for opinions than to ask for cash. Soliciting advice first will help you identify holes in your project idea, strengthen your pitch, and build a relationship. Publicly express gratitude (which must be sincere). When you return having made any suggested changes, your potential investor will likely feel a connection to the initiative and be more favorable to any requests for cash that follow.

EXPLORE EXTERNAL RESOURCES

You can diversify the source of your project resources and gain external legitimacy by seeking assets beyond your work unit or even organization.

No one wants to bear 100 percent of the project risks, and no one wants to feel others are getting a free ride. Look at ways you can share the financial and non-financial burden for your project with other departments or organizations in different sectors. When League Catalyst Justin DeKoszmovszky was an intrapreneur at SC Johnson, he saw the need for greater investment and time to innovate and operate at a scale commensurate with the problems like malaria and poor sanitation that his team was trying to help solve:

> "We built a partnership with the Bill & Melinda Gates Foundation which gave my initiatives 1) major internal cachet, which meant I could 2) get multi-year commitments, and 3) significant philanthropic funds based on the social and health impacts we were delivering."

Now that we've shared general advice on garnering resources, we want to offer some tips on securing additional talent, time, permission, and money for your project.

People

Chapter Three offered tips on how to recruit an intrapreneurial team to guide the project. Ideally, that team possesses all the skills you need to achieve your goal. However, you will likely need additional talents for short-term tasks.

Do your best to understand what motivates the prospective ally and craft a narrative that brings the person to your side. If your organization lacks certain expertise internally, identify players outside your workplace who have a shared interest in seeing the project succeed. Often those players are in your employer's supply or distribution chain, or they may be located in a sector different from yours. Partnerships among government organizations, NGOs, and companies leverage the human capital strengths of each sector while also being able to tackle a complex problem at the systems level.

When Howard Shapiro, the Chief Agricultural Officer at Mars, Inc., became interested in solving the problem of agricultural productivity and nutritional stunting in Africa, he built out some unlikely alliances, recruiting the Mars family as well as a range of cross-sector actors from IBM, the US Department of Agriculture, and West African plant breeders to begin working on the problem. As he remembers, "I collected every kind of outlaw person who I could find who was on the cutting edge of their organization."

Permission

Not all your work projects can be or are ripe for an intrapreneurial approach. Skilled intrapreneurs know how to pick their battles.

For projects that you really care about, you'll need to obtain "intrapreneurial license" from your colleagues. It's easiest to earn this by completing organizationally important projects quickly, thoroughly and, most importantly, just the way your organization wants them. In doing so, your workplace leaders will see that you can deliver for them. Your good track record will make them more receptive to future change ideas.

But, let's say you are running low on "intrapreneurial license." Do you ask for permission to undertake your project? Ideally, you'd have your supervisor's blessing. Some intrapreneurs, however, go rogue and proceed without being explicit about what they're doing. Working in stealth like the "calling janitors" can be effective, but unless your team can make up the missing time at work by volunteering at home, your project is likely to lack an important food category in its diet and be less healthy as a result. If you don't have your boss's permission but you think you can get it elsewhere, look for a sponsor senior to your boss who can advocate for the project and/or create a mandate for you to work on it.

Time

A common myth about intrapreneurs, particularly corporate and government ones, is that they are awash in resources. True, they can sometimes draw on plump organizational budgets; however, intrapreneurs often find themselves very time poor. Already faced with an overflowing task list, they may struggle to find time to work on an intrapreneurial side project even if they theoretically have permission to do so.

You can make time to work on your project and not compromise your job by linking the two together. If your project enhances the quality of work you do now, then time for the project will naturally come throughout the course of your day. If your project falls well outside your day job, you may need to accept duties in the project as a form of volunteer time after hours. If your supervisor and team support the work, you might also find ways to shift work to other teammates in order to free you up.

Consider the case of Mika Turpeinen and Tapio Peltonen, intrapreneurs at ABB. Operating in more than 100 countries, ABB is a technology firm offering a wide range of services including industrial automation, robotics and discrete automation, and electrification. Mika saw an opportunity to increase the penetration of hydropower electricity in rural Ethiopia. Over 80 percent of all the water in the Nile River originates in the country.

Because ABB Finland was developing a new type of permanent magnet generator (for hydro power), he decided to put everything he had toward making this dream come true.

He says that in the first year of the project, "I spent my own free time, holidays and nights, and even some of my own money to study things—meeting up with lots of people and developing ideas further."

Tapio, a consultant on the project, made similar sacrifices: "I worked nearly for a whole year without any compensation from ABB or anyone else … I mean about from half a day to a day in a week during that time, developing the business model and seeking external funding."[45]

If you can't find a way to make the kind of time sacrifices that Mika and Tapio made, be sure to set up a daily routine of at least 10 to 20 minutes to keep the project alive and moving ahead. Alternatively, ask for permission to experiment for a given probationary period.

At some point, you'll likely be told to stop. Gifford Pinchot III describes a common situation encountered in companies:

> "In corporations, new ideas seem to be given a time to reach success. They are tolerated for a while and then they become old news and since they have not produced the results that were hoped for, they are judged to be a failure and terminated. This is a problem because new ideas almost always take longer to reach success than what was originally planned. They may be killed when they are just on the verge of success."[46]

Pinchot recommends some strategies to "restart the clock." For very risky projects, your best bet may be to keep as quiet and unobtrusive as possible. If people aren't thinking about what you're doing, they'll be less likely to wonder whether you should be given more time. Once you have a surprising and good result, announce it and buy yourself another round at the clock.

For higher-visibility projects, build in major milestones like the creation of a prototype or tests you can run. These are milestones that you know you can hit. When you do, you'll offer the project a regular drumbeat of achievement which will allow you to reset the clock over and over.

In the worst case scenario, repackage the project in a way that masks it as something entirely new so that you can keep working on it in another form.

The now ubiquitous Post-it Note almost died of starvation when Art Fry at 3M started running out of time to prove that it had commercial legs. Senior management was unsure what to do with the discovery of the weak glue that made Post-its famous.

For five years, the product went nowhere until a change in management gave Fry a chance to try using the glue for a reusable bulletin board. Product sales were low and it looked like the glue was destined for the graveyard.

But Fry found a way to restart the clock by giving the sticky pads to the administrative assistants of all the company's executives. The assistants fell in love with the product and their bosses began to change their minds, even though Fry hadn't yet figured out how to sell the product to customers.

By resetting the clock this way, the project lived long enough for him to discover the answer. He convinced companies like Hallmark to distribute free Post-it pads to customers with every purchase. Like the administrative assistants, Hallmark's customers couldn't live without the sticky notepads. Almost 90 percent of the companies who received free samples decided to re-order. A whole new product line was born.[47]

Money

The last critical food group for your project is money. By definition, if you're an intrapreneur, you're working in a well-established organization. Most highly-settled communities depend on revenue sources that are cultivated in a well-ordered farming system. If your organization has been around awhile, your farm produces income reliably every season.

That said, budget cuts coming from donors, legislatures, or corporate headquarters may make producing enough revenue more challenging. Invasive species like startups might disrupt a reliable revenue model that has been producing for you every year. You might have outsiders protesting the source of and production methods of your revenue generation. Whatever the situation, you may notice that the old ways of feeding the organization financially are not working as well as they have in the past.

What you're able to forage, hunt, trap, or lure will depend a great deal on the type of ecosystem you're operating in. If it's a resource-rich environment, you'll be able to see the money floating around, but you may struggle to access it because it is trapped in the budgetary canopy at the senior executive level. If you're in a resource-poor environment, money may be hard to come by for everyone, even at the best of times.

Foraging was the first skill that humans mastered in the wilderness, and it's one you'll need to master at the beginning of your project. Foraging for small change that's low to the ground around the office can take the form of asking friendly departments to hand over cash (or discontinued or surplus products) that they have on hand. Ask your fairy godmother for ideas about sources of cash that aren't tied down. When League member Marjorie Brans worked as an intrapreneur at Oxfam America, her mentor and fairy godmother shared a juicy piece of information: a senior manager was toying with the idea of creating an innovation fund. She immediately headed to the manager's office and emerged with $100,000 in startup funds.

Yun Hui Hong, Senior Manager of Corporate Communications at eBay Korea, dreamed of creating a special online store to sell products to meet the needs of older people and people living with disabilities: "I wasn't a product or category manager, so I didn't have the resources to make my idea happen by myself. I needed help from others within eBay."

In 2015, she entered her vision for CarePlus in eBay Korea's Mobile Business Idea Contest. While she didn't win, entering forced her to put her idea to paper. From then on, she gave her elevator pitch to anyone in eBay who might be interested: "Everyone I spoke to liked the idea, but it wasn't their priority. I faced a lot of rejection. I had to stay focused and not give up until I found the right person with the right resources, willing to take the leap with me."

Two years and seven rejections later, she found a colleague willing to back her: Soon Suk Kim, one of the company's auction platform category managers. He believed in the market potential of CarePlus and in Yun Hui's personal passion for the project. He put up the money to build the website and it grew from there.[48]

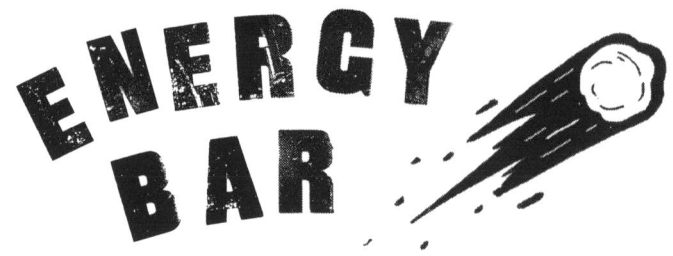

RAJ AND SKARP ON GOING ROGUE

Two social intrapreneurs at Nokia, known as Raj and Skarp, wanted to establish an intrapreneurial business called VilCo in India. The purpose of the unit would be to extend access to innovative and low-cost cell phone technology to remote villages in India where a traditional technology and business model would not make for a profitable business.

The pair set out to make it happen, but not far into the project, an established business unit at Nokia began to worry that this intrapreneurial project would cannibalize the existing market. One of the intrapreneurs was told, "This is not what you should be doing; you will take the bread out of our mouth."

Undeterred, the two intrapreneurs began working on the project on their own time: "Raj and I were incredibly passionate about this ... normally if the boss says no way, you obey. Your attitude is: I only work here and someone else tells me what to do. But [in VilCo] we thought we had this innovation and we wanted to carry on ... we can overcome any obstacles, let's just keep going ... Money certainly wasn't the motivation; we never saw any bonuses or anything like that."

Similarly, Raj shared Skarp's passion for the project and the opportunity for public service:

"It was definitely a very different experience because we were creating a new business model along with new technology to meet real user needs, and it was also by far the most rewarding experience ever: VilCo meant that many tens of thousands of people living in remote rural parts of the world would be making their very first phone call."[49]

KAUSHIK SRIDHAR ON LEVERAGING START-UP FUNDS

Kaushik is a member of the League of Intrapreneurs in Australia where he works for one of Australia's largest aged care companies as a National Sustainability Manager.

Kaushik is responsible for developing and implementing the company's first-ever sustainability strategy. His goal is to integrate sustainability into the core of the business in ways that transform the company. With a new mandate and "a blank piece of canvas to paint on," Kaushik needed to establish quickly that he could get this new strategy off the ground.

During a government workshop for the country's leading healthcare companies, Kaushik saw an opportunity to engage both the public and private sectors in the broader vision of improving healthcare outcomes for Australians. There was just one hitch: he needed startup funds. Kaushik proposed a modest $20,000 in seed funds to the federal government, and to his pleasant surprise, the proposal was successful.

Kaushik's bold but modest ask earned him respect from his company and demonstrated that he was willing to pursue every avenue and creative partnerships to realize the company goal. This early win inspired other departments to make investments in line with the sustainability plan. Kaushik estimates that they have spent at least $200,000 in additional startup activities out of budgets that he doesn't control, but that advance the goals his team helped inspire. Engaging a broad range of colleagues across the organization is evidenced in a non-financial way as well. This year, over 200 people submitted nominations for company awards that reward action on sustainability goals. Last year, that number was just 10.

Feeding Your Project for Growth and Scale

Over time, low-calorie startup and seed funds will cause your project to starve. Past the initial stages of intrapreneurial activity, you'll need to round out your diet with protein-heavy development funds that allow your project to mature. Sometimes you will have to scrounge for bait around the office. For instance, if marketing isn't your forte, a volunteer hour or two from your office's graphic designer and communications team can take your pitch deck from blah to brilliant.

Remember, if you don't succeed with one tactic, try another. You'll have to design something appropriate for the operating context and the personalities involved. An intelligently designed set of strategies has the potential to trap more resources than a single big ask that fails.

Leverage industry-wide movement toward sustainable practices; paint a colorful picture of the future; repeat conversations you've heard at competitor organizations. Coupled with a strong business or impact case, you will be well on your way to securing the organizational assets you need.

Transforming an intrapreneurial project into a going concern and even to a profitable venture is no easy feat, but it can be done. Many intrapreneurs rely on the Business Model Canvas to identify sustainable revenue streams. New hybrid sources of funding are emerging, such as the UK's Department for International Development's Business Partnerships Fund. And governments like the EU are allocating billions to address mission-critical issues like climate change and food security. Theoretically you will have access to your organization's brand assets and infrastructure as a foundation, potentially giving you a big head start.

For instance, WWF's Landscape Finance Lab, established in April 2016 by intrapreneur Paul Chatterton, is creating impact at a scale most environmental NGOs can only dream of. The Lab focuses exclusively on projects covering over a million hectares, a million tons of traded goods, a million tons of greenhouse gases, and $100 million in investment size.

Taking advantage of a new generation of environmentally-focused investment funds like the Green Climate Fund and the Land Degradation Neutrality Fund, financing for these types of projects has increased from the standard $1 million to $10 million range to $50 million to $250 million. The Landscape Finance Lab tests new project financing pathways.

WWF's largest investment in one location is the Mai Ndombe Emission Reduction Program in the Democratic Republic of Congo. The project was established to save millions of hectares of moist tropical forests, and has $170 million in funding from the World Bank Carbon Fund to do so.

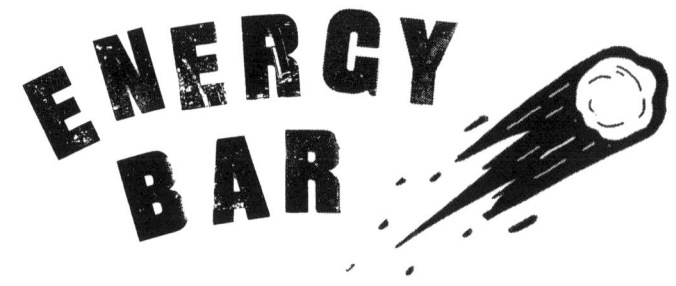

VAL THOMAS ON FORAGING
DEVELOPMENT & SCALING FUNDS

Capture Canada is a Creative Commons photo-sharing app showcasing Canada's diversity through beautiful, royalty-free photos. Val Thomas led its creation after she won an innovation contest for Canadian federal government intrapreneurs (out of more than 500 entries).

There was one hitch: the award came with no money or resources to build the app. Undaunted, Val convinced her boss to let her spend six months fundraising and prototyping. She created a business plan, mobilized key stakeholders, and went out and began pitching the idea as a startup. She approached various departments with tin cup in hand asking them to direct these monies to Ingenium—Canada's Museums of Science and Innovation. As a Crown corporation, the museum could run a multi-year project with greater flexibility. As a result, Val foraged enough dollars to create a seed fund for the app, allowing it to continue to this day.

CATALYZING INTRAPRENEURSHIP AT BNP PARIBAS

For more than five years, French banking giant BNP Paribas' #Intrapreneurs4Good program has been bringing together "calling janitor" personalities to initiate projects that will help the company identify opportunities for innovation, new markets, and social good.

#Intrapreneurs4Good taps into the idealism of the company's employees globally. In 2019, over 150 teams applied to the program and 12 projects were selected to tackle different aspects of the UN SDGs. Offering 20 days of training over four months, BNP Paribas helps its intrapreneurs develop their ideas, attract internal sponsors, and finance startup costs. The company also allows participants to take time to work on their projects.

According to company representative Sandrine Delage, the program not only tackles important social challenges, but it also offers employees an opportunity to change their mindsets and ways of working: "each intrapreneur reaches an average of 100 persons at work. They become levers for more agile and 4Good organization and spirit at the core of the company and beyond: in their respective ecosystems."

BNP Paribas is part of a growing group of companies investing in intrapreneurs. SAP has launched its One Billion Lives accelerator to harness SAP's technology to improve the lives of billions. Danone's Ecosystem Fund has given rise to a multitude of intrapreneurial ventures. Governments and NGOs are starting to tap this potential as well: CARE, UNICEF, and UNHCR have established innovation units, while the World Bank runs an intrapreneurial competition offering winners $100,000 to test out new ideas.[50]

Last-Ditch Tactics

As mentioned earlier, intrapreneurship as an idea is growing in popularity among senior managers across all three sectors. In workplaces where it has been adopted as an innovation strategy, we are seeing more and more funding pots being allocated to intrapreneurial projects.

If you're unable to secure support for your social venture specifically, consider pushing for intrapreneurship as a general concept. Your idea might be a little too fresh and bold for management now, but management may grow to like it once they've had a taste of more modest and different examples of innovation.

You can point to organizations as diverse as Barclays, Cemex, Pearson,[51] the US Federal Communications Commission,[52] the Australian Federal Government, and NGOs like CARE and Comic Relief that are all promoting social intrapreneurship as a concept. In doing so, talk about the various approaches:

– Holding pitch events for intrapreneurial projects

– A physical space where intrapreneurs can gather and connect

– Hackathons or innovation sprints that get the creative juices going

– Giving employees a little free time to work on their ideas

An indirect attempt to create more appetite for innovation may improve the environment for your project down the line.

Staying Psychologically Hydrated

Water is crucial to life. Without water, the body's cells begin to die after only two to three days. Skimping on water on a daily basis leads to high blood pressure and kidney stones. As you work on your challenging intrapreneurial venture, drink lots of water. And we mean actual water. Your brain and body will simply work better.

Your mind equally needs hydration, especially if you're operating in a toxic work environment. Psychological and spiritual desiccation will impair the circulation of project lifeblood, making your heart work harder to pump it. Weakness, nausea, irritability, headaches, and dizziness are all symptoms of physical (and sometimes spiritual) dehydration. Look for signs of dehydration in yourself and your companions. If you see signs, rehydrate immediately.

In intrapreneurship, your biggest challenge may be finding water that's clean enough to drink. When you propose an idea that is counter to the culture of the organization, you may be attacked and you might feel that the office is a toxic place where it is hard to keep your mind psychologically healthy.

Teresa Sivilli and Thaddeus Pace of the Garrison Institute have studied the human dimensions of resilience. From this research, the League identified five key traits applicable to the practice of intrapreneurship. We share these with you on the next page.

Human Dimensions of Resilience

(Adapted for social intrapreneurs from the Garrison Institute)

Resilience, n. "the ability to bounce back after stress, and to remain minimally disturbed by a given amount of stress. Psychological resilience is defined by flexibility in response to changing situational demands, and the ability to bounce back from negative emotional experiences."[53]

1. BUILD YOUR CAPACITY TO COPE WITH STRESS

If you are sincere in your desire to change the world for the better, you will likely grow weary and despair when the world does not yield easily to your efforts. Realize that most people are just doing their best. Practice compassion for your colleagues. They are trying to get by, operating on the career management logic that has been inculcated in them since childhood. When you come along questioning their ways of doing things, they will have good reason to reject it. After all, you're asking them to abandon things they know work well, or at least well enough. Social intrapreneurship is about bringing more love and kindness into the world; view resistance as an opportunity to practice what you preach. The more that people sense your good intentions, the more they are likely to hear you out.

But when things get tough, shut your computer down for a few days, take a vacation, or meditate. Sanjiv Chopra, the former Dean of Harvard Medical School, counsels people to meditate daily. He adds, "And if you don't have time to do that, you should meditate twice a day." Try meditating in the morning before you head to the office. When you need a pick me up, find a quiet corner, or listen to a guided meditation recording for five minutes at your desk. Headspace or similar meditation apps are a good place to start.

2. ASK FOR HELP

Intrapreneurs often fail to ask for help. As high-capacity people, they are often the people that others turn to for assistance. You don't need to be a superhero, and in fact, we strenuously discourage you from trying to be one. Ask colleagues for help, if for no other reason than it gives them a chance to contribute and feel ownership over your intrapreneurial endeavor. They may not do things as well as you or as fast as you, but remember that the bigger goal is to bring about culture change. Asking for help affords your officemates an opportunity to practice a new way of moving through the workplace with higher consciousness.

SLOW MOVING INSTITUTIONAL BEAST

3. MOVE FROM "ME" TO "WE"

Asking for help should come from a place of solidarity. When you see that your intrapreneurial teammates are struggling, take them out for a walk in the park. Participate in or create a circle of trust with peers who aren't there to solve technical challenges, but to offer a supportive space to one another. Join the League of Intrapreneurs as individuals or a group. Sometimes finding acknowledgement or generating momentum as a group can be just what is needed to gain internal traction.

4. BELIEVE IN YOURSELF

When you feel like you're drowning in toxic waters, restore your sense of confidence by focusing on your self-esteem. Nathaniel Branden's masterpiece *The Six Pillars of Self-Esteem* offers deep theory and very practical exercises on how to decouple your sense of self-worth from the approval of others. As you begin to operate by a logic of achievement that places higher emphasis on benefit to humanity and the planet, others will question your idea of success. They will say that you shouldn't do things that might get you fired or compromise your next promotion. A strong sense of self and your values will buoy your spirits as a vortex of negativity swirls around you.

5. OPERATE FROM YOUR HIGHEST SELF

Reconnect with your sense of purpose and non-negotiable. When times get tough, you'll want to remember why you set out on this pathfinding journey in the first place.

ENERGY BAR

GIB BULLOCH ON HOW TO FOCUS ON BEING, NOT JUST DOING

Gib Bulloch, author of *The Intrapreneur: Confessions of a Corporate Insurgent* and board member of the League of Intrapreneurs, was the driving force behind Accenture's "not-for-loss" consulting arm ADP (first mentioned on page 72). Here he shares his views on resilience:

> "On the face of it, I'm probably not the best person to talk about resilience, having found myself taking an unexpected 'short break' in a psychiatric ward in Glasgow in 2014. I'd always considered myself fairly robust—I loved the job I was doing, felt reasonably secure in it, had no major money or personal worries. Burnout, anxiety, or other mental health issues were for other people to worry about. Or so I thought. But it turned out I wasn't bulletproof. The daily pressures of the corporate immune system inevitably took their toll. A bad fever picked up in India might have been a catalyst, but I certainly hadn't seen it coming.
>
> Often we learn more from our failures or setbacks than we do from our successes. Five years on I've learned that preventative maintenance is the key. Rather than wait until your car breaks down, it's better to have routine check ups and provide some regular TLC. Similarly, these days I'll try to drink less, eat better, and engage in activities like yoga or meditation to balance the 'being' with most people's default focus on the doing."

DON'T GET CAUGHT OUT!
Familiarize yourself with common obstacles
and challenges of the journey.

6

Survival Tips & Techniques

While intrapreneurial pathfinding can provide beautiful, inspiring, and memorable experiences, it can also surprise you in less pleasant ways. Master these life-saving techniques and before you know it, you will be a more skilled intrapreneur—and most importantly, one who survived to tell the tale!

Help! I'm Overwhelmed!

By definition, innovative projects are ones that involve doing something that the current system isn't set up to do. This fact invariably means that as you move toward your destination, you will likely have violated a current rule, role, or operating method in the process. Innovation is inherently about traversing boundaries. Sometimes this happens by accident and other times, intentionally.

When crossing boundaries, you'll wander into terrain that is unfamiliar and that may feel dangerous. These boundaries can be personal or professional ones. You may need to learn the ways of another sector, to operate above your "pay grade" and title, to master new areas of professional expertise, or to reveal personal vulnerabilities and passions when you've likely been trained to guard that information behind the lines of your professional persona.

With each boundary crossing, ask yourself if you're in your comfort zone, stretch zone, or panic zone. The comfort zone is a place of familiarity. The human brain is designed to avoid surprises (who knows if those bushes are rustling because it's a tiger or a child?). This preference for certainty is so deeply ingrained that many people will choose a bad situation they know over a potentially great situation they don't know.

No wonder we often say, "Better the devil you know than the devil you don't."

Your overriding value as an intrapreneur is your capacity to move into the unknown where it is, by definition, possible to be surprised for good or for ill. This is the "stretch zone," the area of growth and innovation. Try to keep your team in this area.

Beyond the sphere of the stretch zone is the "panic zone," the place where a person feels a goal is too far away to be attainable but is still required as a target. The panic zone is the area on the mental map that, according to legend, ancient cartographers labeled with "HC SVNT DRACONES" or, "here be dragons" to signify the lands that were unknown and terrifying. In the panic zone, you and your team will experience the fear and stress that comes from feeling completely out of control over your fate. All your energy will be redirected to regaining control and not on doing things that contribute to team well-being and innovation.

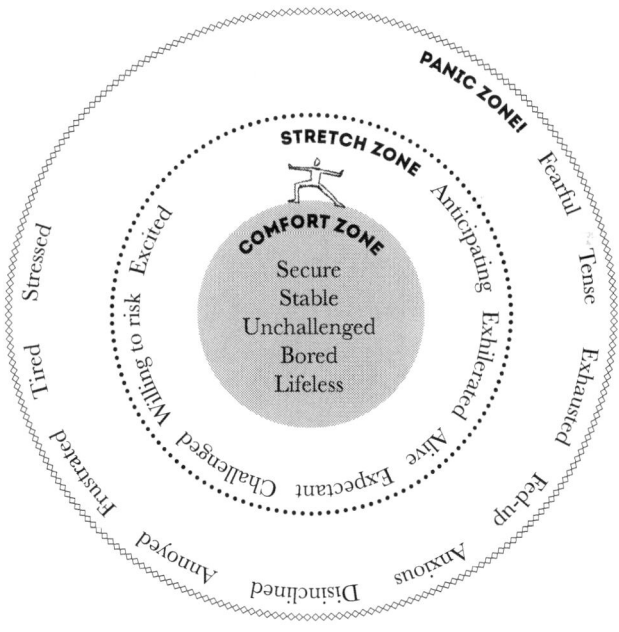

Fig. 10. The Learning Zone model. Adapted from Tom Senninger, 2004. Abenteuer leiten, in Abenteuern lernen. BBS Buchwerk Bernard Schön. https://digitalacademicblog.wordpress.com/tag/senningers-learning-zone-model/.

It is important to realize that people's zone thresholds are different, and that they may vary by situation. They may also change over time as people stretch toward greater levels of service to the world. In his book *The Second Mountain*, author and cultural commentator David Brooks describes two types of metaphorical mountains that people climb.[54] Most adults eventually find themselves climbing the "first mountain" of conventional success that leads to so-called happiness. The problem is that when they arrive at the top, the view feels unsatisfying and they decide they should climb somewhere else. The "second mountain" is where people realize that a life worth living embraces interdependence, purpose, and commitment to serving other people. Many of the League's most experienced intrapreneurs quickly climbed the first mountain at the office, only to realize that their lives lacked joy and that they needed something else.

As you invite your colleagues to join you on a second mountain climb, realize that some of your co-travelers (and possibly yourself included) might be climbing the first mountain in the mistaken belief that they are on the second. Knowing the difference is a matter of experience and consciousness. As the terrain of social innovation becomes more familiar, you'll develop a better sense of where you are on the mental map.

Help! I'm Feeling Attacked and Stressed

"It is no measure of health to be well adjusted to a profoundly sick society." J. Krishnamurti

If "they're not getting me" is starting to feel more like "they're out to get me," know that it's not you … it's actually you, them, and the grey matter between our ears.

In his book *Deviate: The Science of Seeing Differently*, neuroscientist Beau Lotto explains how our entire perceptual system evolved to avoid death by eliminating uncertainty–uncertainty about what lies in the dark bushes (a baby from our village or a jaguar?). Yet, paradoxically, the human race has flourished thanks to those who embrace uncertainty:

"When you are sitting in your community, sheltered and protected, where everything is momentarily predictable, the last thing you want to do is say, 'Hmmmm, I wonder what is on the other side of the hill?' Bad idea! The probability of dying just suddenly increased considerably. But it is because of that 'mad' individual that the group has a better chance to survive in an environment that is dynamic—by learning what dangers or benefits are on the other side of that hill, and perhaps discovering new spaces of possibility that the group hadn't known existed."[55]

Consider for a moment that as a social intrapreneur, your function in the system is to behave like the "mad" community member who is encouraging the village to travel over the next horizon. In most workplaces, very few people will jump up immediately to join you—biology is simply not on your side. As neuroscientist Robert Sapolsky writes in *Behave: The Biology of Humans at Our Best and Worst*:

"The depths of human conformity and obedience are shown by the speed with which they occur—it takes less than 200 milliseconds for your brain to register that the group has picked a different answer from yours, and less than 380 milliseconds for a profile of activation that predicts changing your opinion. Our brains are biased to get along by going along in less than a second."[56]

In taking on an intrapreneurial project, realize that you're exhibiting non-conforming, disruptive behavior that conflicts with the biological tendency to go with the flow. In asking people implicitly or explicitly to take on professional risks with unclear chances of success, you're signing up for a situation of resistance.

If you've come to a point in your intrapreneurial endeavor where you and those around you are stressed by your venture, tread carefully. Sapolsky explains that "stress can disrupt cognition, impulse control, emotional regulation, decision making, empathy, and prosociality." Note that this statement applies not only to "them" but to you too.

The good news is just as science helps explain our instincts to stick to what we know, it can also help you and your colleagues to navigate your way out of this hairy situation by moving into a more productive and cooperative mental state. Here we look at proven methods to help you:

– Manage your own stress and insecurities.

– Minimize uncertainty in others and facilitate their self-empowerment.

Manage Your Own Stress and Insecurities

Instead of feeling like the hero on this journey, you get the sense that people are attacking you. For anyone identifying with these words in a real life intrapreneurial emergency, Google's researcher on empathy and emotional intelligence Peter Jin Hong draws on insights from behavioral neuroscience to explain what has probably happened:

– They can't see what you see, which you think is obvious.

– They question it, so you start questioning it and doubting yourself.

– They can't relate. They feel criticized and threatened.

– They make you feel like you're crazy.

– They start to pull away, a passive reaction.

– They start to push you away, an active reaction.

If this sounds about right, stop what you're doing and take these steps:

Breathe deeply to reduce the hormonal alarm bells going off in your head. Our noses clean, humidify, and regulate the temperature of the air that we breathe. When we breathe deeply through our nose, our sinuses create nitric oxide which kills off unwanted bacteria and viruses in our body. Nose breathing also stimulates the parasympathetic nerve receptors in the lower lung which are associated with calming of the body. [57]

Sleep on it. Intrapreneurship is about tackling very complex problems by creatively recombining institutional assets into new solutions. Brain research suggests that sleep is critical not only to health, but also to creativity. Scientist Penny Lewis of Cardiff University hypothesizes that rapid-eye movement (REM) and non-REM sleep work together to help the brain find patterns and commonalities between seemingly unrelated phenomena. She likens these two sleep cycles to "two researchers who initially work on the same problem together, then go away and each think about it separately, then come back together to work on it further … The obvious implication is that if you're working on a difficult problem, allow yourself enough nights of sleep … Particularly if you're trying to work on something that requires thinking outside the box."[58]

Meditate and practice gratitude. Hong also says the key to pulling out of the stress death loop is to remember that your colleagues are not your enemies; they are members of your village, and the worst thing you can do is to start seeing them as "other." Invoke a sense of gratitude to your workmates for all the things they are doing right. The science of empathy research has shown that in addition to deep breathing, mindfulness, and cultivating gratitude can make a practical difference in behavior, mood, and brain physiology. In mindful, grateful states, our brains release gamma aminobutyric acid (GABA), a naturally occurring amino acid that works as a neurotransmitter in your brain. With more GABA, you will experience greater patience, be more open to opposing views, and experience greater willingness to cooperate and build with people you may see as opponents. You will also put the brakes on runaway dopamine and cortisol (the stress hormone).

In *The Upside of Stress*, Stanford psychologist Kelly McGonigal points out that stress can be beneficial when embraced versus avoided at all costs.[59] McGonigal counsels people to understand stress as a helpful energy boost in a challenging situation. Stress is a natural part of life and can be something your body is fully capable of handling under the right circumstances. McGonigal says, "Stress is most likely to be harmful when the following conditions are present: it feels against your will, out of your control and utterly devoid of meaning."[60]

Given that a social intrapreneurial project is all about meaning, you're in a great position to see the stress you're feeling as something that is working in service to a cause greater than yourself.

Minimize uncertainty in others and focus on self-empowerment

Our workplace is a system embedded in a larger system that values profit at any cost and lifeless objects over healthy relationships and planetary flourishing. Your values are not centered in most workplaces. But know that many people come to the office with those values too—they just may not know how to make them manifest in the day-to-day, given current unhealthy workplace expectations and incentive structures. A fear-based response to your colleague's fear will get in the way of collaboration.

Most people are just trying to get by. When people are afraid, they struggle to solve complex problems like gender bias or racism. Increasingly urgent calls from external stakeholders for change may generate a siege mentality among your colleagues. Neuroscientists have found that when people experience negative sensations like the feeling of being attacked, they also experience a decline in cognitive function.

Psychologist Daniel Goleman coined the term "amygdala hijack" in his seminal text *Emotional Intelligence: Why it Can Matter More than IQ*.[61] As Hong explains, "the amygdala is the so-called 'lizard brain,' the oldest and most emotional part of our brain that is responsible for triggering a fight or flight response. When our lizard brain senses a threat (e.g., uncertainty or stress), it can trigger within .380 milliseconds (less than a blink of an eye) the HPA (hypothalmic-pituitary-adrenal) axis that causes us to act irrationally before our prefrontal cortex and 'wizard' brain can kick in to regulate the reaction."

Conversely, a study of clinical reasoning among practicing physicians found that when the doctors were first given a bag of candy to prime them for positive effect, they were 19 percent quicker to consider the correct diagnosis and were much less prone to "anchoring" (defined as "distortion or inflexibility in thinking"), compared to a control group. Neuropsychologists Gregory Ashby, Alice Isen, and And Turken theorize that increased brain dopamine levels associated with positive emotions lead to consolidation of long-term memories, working memory, and creative problem solving, because "increased dopamine release in the anterior cingulate improves cognitive flexibility and facilitates the selection of cognitive perspective."[62]

Once you've moved back into a space of collaboration, you can help your colleagues do the same. You'll need to go back to the basics. Robert Sapolsky advises anyone locked into an "us versus them" battle to:

– Emphasize what you have in common.

– Find value in other's perspectives.

– Find more benign dichotomies.

– Reduce hierarchical differences.

– Bring everyone together on equal terms with shared goals.[63]

In an intrapreneurial context, here's how you might put these principles into action.

Dissolve the boundaries between you and your colleagues

Commit to eradicating unhelpful dichotomies in your mind and your speech.

Sapolsky points out that humans learn to dichotomize the world from early on, usually with no ill intent: "When a kindergarten teacher says, 'Good morning, boys and girls,' the kids are being taught that dividing the world that way is more meaningful than saying, 'Good morning, those of you who have lost a tooth and those of you who haven't yet.'"[64]

Dichotomies pervade our lives and we naturally use them to navigate social behavior and our world. But sometimes those dichotomies can turn into othering that creates enemies. In your project, you may be thinking "there are those of us who are moral and there are those of us who are heartless, greedy bastards."

Thinking this way will not advance your project because you will behave and communicate in ways that unconsciously betray your othering judgement. A perhaps more productive way to think of the difference between you and your detractors is more subtle. Think about "those who see what you see" versus "those who have not yet seen what you see."

Launch a diplomacy tour

Now that you're in the right mindspace, you can call forth your inner diplomat and bridge-building skills. Your "tour" is a concentrated effort to learn what you've missed, help people see what you see, and explore how your collective goals can be joined up. Start by setting up meetings individually with those people where you sense a gap. Don't wait for them to come to you. Show that you're ready to have the difficult conversation and engage with them first.

Start by learning what you haven't yet seen from your colleagues' perspectives. Listening actively is the cornerstone of empathy. Ask open-ended questions about their objections to explore what people have to say (see page 85 again for helpful language). Play back literally what you're hearing and allow others to be fully heard. Silence your natural defensive responses and just listen.

You need to understand the gaps they are seeing in your project (and understand that a gap may simply be that it makes people uncomfortable). You haven't done your job until you've met their needs, priorities, and motivations too. Acknowledge where you agree with people and mention how their input has made you think differently.

Now ask what goals your colleagues' have for themselves and the organization. Ask them what goals they think you should be meeting. With all of these puzzle pieces in front of you, you can begin to treat the gap between you as a puzzle to solve together as partners. Don't try to solve it all at once. Thank your colleague for the conversation and say you will take what they've said and mull it over and suggest a way forward.

Invite others to "own" the solution

Now that you've properly acknowledged that you've heard your colleagues and you've taken the time to take their critiques on board, you may have come to a new point of view. This is not to suggest that you give up on your lofty goals, but that you will have come to an appreciation of the pressures that are getting in the way.

At this point, consider convening a group discussion where you can lay all the puzzle pieces in front of the group and ask how you can put them together. Half of making the business case is getting others to make it for you–invite others to do some of the heavy lifting by examining how your project could support the goals of the broader group. We highly recommend reading the elegant and powerful book *Getting to Yes: How To Negotiate Agreement Without Giving In* by Roger Fisher and William Ury. In this manual, you will learn the habits of thought and process of professional diplomats and find that it allows you to reach wise agreements.

Find ways to emphasize your shared humanity

While you work to de-risk your idea and build a credible case, we also encourage you to find ways to inspire your colleagues and create space for them to tap into their potential for compassion and awe. Dacher Keltner of the University of Berkeley's Greater Good Science Center says that awe is "the feeling of being in the presence of something vast that transcends your understanding of the world."[65] It is a sensation inspired by art, nature, and acts of great skill or virtue, such as when we get chills listening to a symphony, are immersed in a spectacular mountain setting, or upon seeing a stranger help a homeless person. Unlike other positive emotions like pride or amusement, awe shifts the human psyche toward more prosocial collaborative ways. In one study, Michelle Shiota asked two groups of participants to complete the sentence "I am ____." Group One looked at an awe-inspiring T. rex skeleton, while Group Two looked down a hallway.[66] Shiota found that Group One was statistically more likely to identify themselves in terms of a common culture, species, university or moral cause than Group Two.[67]

The lesson? Try using a benevolent form of the old military tactic known as "shock and awe" to highlight your common humanity. Strategic experiences of awe through art, nature, and lofty human behavior may short circuit negative dynamics in your team, and allow you all to get back to common ground. Think about how you can connect with your teammates as human beings in the collective of our species—hold the next discussion at an especially delicious restaurant, or museum, or nature retreat; find someone to compose an inspiring song about your idea; or invite respected peers who have changed the world to speak with your colleagues. Through awe, we gain an understanding of our individual smallness and the beauty of being part of a collective.

At the end of the day, you can't control your colleagues' reactions, but you can control yours. The more you bring calm and compassion to the situation, the better you'll inspire cooperation, and—with luck and hope—jointly, you'll find the awe of working together on a project of great meaning.

MAU PIAILUG ON BELIEVING IN YOURSELF

In 1975, Micronesian navigator Mau Piailug demonstrated how ancient Polynesians likely managed to make the round trip between Hawai'i and Tahiti and other long distances using the rising points of the stars, observations of the ocean swells, and flight patterns of sea birds. Employing a future-backcasting technique that would rival if not surpass the magician Merlin, he navigated easily even on days where solid cloud cover obscured the stars, sun, and moon. Introducing the technique to Nainoa Thompson, a novice navigator at the time, he offered this lesson as recounted by Nainoa:

> "In November of 1979, Mau and I went to observe the sky at Lana'i Lookout. We would leave for Tahiti soon. I was concerned—more like a little bit afraid. It was an awesome challenge. Then he asked, 'Can you point to the direction of Tahiti?' I pointed. Then he asked, 'Can you see the island?' I was puzzled by the question. Of course I could not actually see the island; it was over 2,200 miles away. But the question was a serious one. I had to consider it carefully. Finally, I said, 'I cannot see the island but I can see an image of the island in my mind.' Mau said, 'Good. Don't ever lose that image or you will be lost.' Then he turned to me and said, 'Let's get in the car, let's go home.' That was the last lesson. Mau was telling me that I had to trust myself and that if I had a vision of where I wanted to go and held onto it, I would get there."[68]

Help! I've Lost My Confidence!

Sometimes, intrapreneurs receive so much pushback that they lose their way and their sense of confidence. If this happens to you, there are two important things to focus on:

Your inner voice—the things you say to yourself that either boost your self-belief or discourage you.

The people you surround yourself with—those who give you permission to be confident and remind you of your gifts.

If you find that you or your team has lost confidence, before you start fleeing back toward the familiar and comfortable, just **STOP:**

S Sit and calm yourself. The part of your brain that controls goal-seeking, such as the desire to move out of a place of confusion back into the familiar, is tied up with emotions.

A strong emotional reaction tends to trump rational thought. Wise intrapreneurs respond to the urge to take knee-jerk action by harnessing that emotional energy and channeling it in constructive ways. Don't simply return to doing business as usual because you aren't sure how to move ahead.

T Think about how you got here, and how you can get out.

O Observe what is around you and what you can leverage. This is a good time to remember your purpose and why you started this project in the first place. Measure where you are in relation to that. Can you increase your elevation to zoom out and see the bigger picture?

P Plan your next move carefully (or possibly plan to stay in place and signal for rescue from the fairy godmother you recruited in Chapter Three). Your fairy godmother may not actually have magical powers, but she or he can intervene as a mentor when you're really unsure of yourself. Keep your godmother informed on the project and reach out when you need help.

I Don't Have Enough Resources

Intrapreneurship requires more than just a generative mindset. You also need a healthy dose of resourcefulness. The old saying, "scarcity is the mother of invention," rings true today for the social intrapreneur as much as it did for our prehistoric ancestors. Today, the ability to improvise from nothing is part of the animating zeitgeist of makers, do-it-yourself-ers, and lean startup enthusiasts.

Thought you had an approved budget for your intrapreneurial project, and now you don't? Trying to shake funds out of the system's tree canopy and no fruit has fallen to the ground? You can often find an improvised solution that helps you adapt to and quickly overcome the obstacle.

These "frugal innovation" approaches draw on the concept of *jugaad*, a Hindi word meaning makeshift and informal innovation that involves the construction or creation of a work from whatever happens to be available. Authors Simone Ahuja, Navi Radjou, and Jaideep Prabhu have studied how innovation happens in the most resource-scarce environments like India. In their book, *Jugaad Innovation*, they offer six principles for the jugaad innovator.[69]

Six principles for the jugaad innovator:

1. Seek opportunity from adversity

2. Do more with less

3. Think and act flexibly

4. Keep it simple

5. Include the margins (of society)

6. Follow your heart

British journalist Dean Nelson, author of *Jugaad Yatra: Exploring the Indian Art of Problem Solving*, recounts the story of an ice-based cooling machine called the "Snowbreeze." Invented by a retired Indian journalist to address the needs of people living in rural poverty, the device is very cheap and its humble origins apparent: "It was a large blue plastic dustbin with a raised lid mounted on an aquamarine skateboard."

Another example of jugaad thinking in service to rural communities comes from Vortex Engineering Private Limited which invented the Gramateller ATM, an automated bank teller that uses the equivalent energy of a 70-watt light bulb. Despite costing only a quarter of the price of average ATMs, it offers fingerprint authentication for users who cannot read and battery power capable of handling the country's frequent power outages. Because bank machines are often hundreds of miles away from a given village, the Gramateller is an indispensible jugaad innovation designed through inexpensive trial-and-error experiments.[70]

Next time you are feeling the pinch, mentally empty every asset of your team onto the floor and examine them to discover new ways in which they can be directed. Your spirits will soar when you figure out an alternative way to get what you need.

CHAPTER SIX

I Feel Like Quitting

As an intrapreneur, you face the distinct possibility (if not probability) that some individuals will feel your project is being poorly led. Alternatively, you may not be getting any traction and you've heard "no" more times than you can count. If you find yourself in such a situation, you may contemplate quitting.

Quitting or not quitting may be one of the hardest decisions you will ever make.

It is important to be able to distinguish whether you are at a dead end or at a dip in the curve. This is the time to call on your fairy godmother or peers for advice and wise counsel.

For some intrapreneurial ventures, the solution may be to spin out. For example, Physic Ventures, a leading impact investor, exists in part to a spinout of Unilever's Technology Ventures. Similarly, Amit Mehra spun out Reuters Market Light into a standalone social enterprise when he reached the limits of scale within his corporate host.

For other ventures, you may find that you are able to have more systems impact from another platform. Take for instance Daniel Vennard, the intrapreneur at Mars we mentioned earlier. Recognizing that he needed to focus on shifting food systems away from a focus on meat to plant-based protein, he chose to leave the private sector and move to the NGO, World Resources Institute, where he could act as a convener across the industry to better unlock systems solutions.

Before you make the leap, our League community suggests a few helpful questions for reflection:

– Have you asked for what you truly need? If the choice is between leaving the company or taking a risk with a big ask, why not take the risk? The answer may surprise you.

– Can you re-energize without quitting? Is there an option for a sabbatical?

168

- Is there a better platform within the company from which to make this change?

- How much risk can you afford personally? Take care not to put yourself in a situation where achieving your goals might be even further away than before.

- Is the grass really greener? Can you practice "appreciative inquiry" and look at all the benefits and positives and what you might lose in making the leap?

If you opt to leave the comfort of an established organization to become an entrepreneur, expect emotional destabilization.

There is inherent turmoil in realizing you're on your own. However, many social intrapreneurs find the time as entrepreneurs a welcome period to recharge and run free without the constraints of bureaucracy.

One League intrapreneur asked not to be identified as he is in the middle of deciding whether to quit or not. The very unexpected and sudden layoff of his direct supervisor prompted this intrapreneur to examine whether his current organization is the right place to continue his quest. The supervisor had been a great executive champion for the intrapreneur's project and now that she is gone, the intrapreneur is wondering whether it would be better to try his luck elsewhere.

"The layoff happened less than a week after I completed my fellowship program with the League, so the coincidental timing really had me thinking about the alignment of my job and my purpose. I was simultaneously feeling pumped up from my time with other intrapreneurs and very uncertain about what was in store for my work unit.

I've learned that the reorganization initiated by our CEO will take six to eight months to complete, so now I'm in a wait-and-see mode. I view this period a bit like a 'freeze-thaw-refreeze' cycle. When things were in a really steady 'frozen' state, it was hard to make change. But we're currently in a period of thaw where the situation is fluid, and there might be an opportunity to shape the future into something really positive. I'm currently doing my best to get comfortable with the organizational ambiguity and forge relationships with other project champions in the senior management team. In fact, one of those champions just became my new boss. We'll see. I'm still figuring things out and am hoping that I can influence things so that they will refreeze in a way that I can feel good about (or at least good enough to keep pushing my project)."

How Do I Survive Mortal Peril?

Intrapreneurship inherently involves taking risks, and with risk comes the possibility for failure and an understandable desire to hide away from the gaze of our colleagues. When we fail to achieve something that is important to us, there are two ways to interpret it:

1. As a sign that we tried something hard and worthwhile, but our efforts came up short.

2. As a sign that we didn't fail on this initiative, but rather, we are a failure as a person.

Internalizing failure as an assessment of our character can turn failure into a source of toxic shame.

Shame on its own is an interesting phenomenon. It is one of the human emotions that can be dysfunctional and functional at the same time.[71] The Old English word hama means a veil or covering, and is the root for the word shame.

When we experience shame as a result of failing ourselves (i.e., not living up to our own standards for behavior or values), then shame may be a justified emotion, one that points to the gap between the person we are now and the person we want to be. In that sense, shame can be productive if we learn from it.

Toxic shame, however, is harmful when it comes from the negative self-assessment that we are deficient as a person. In a social intrapreneurial context, toxic shame can result from an intrapreneur trying to push the organization to take a risk toward realizing its higher self. When these efforts fail, colleagues are likely to start pointing fingers at you and saying you have compromised everyone's security.

Consider the 2017 Pepsi ad featuring supermodel, Kendall Jenner, in a television spot that borrowed imagery from the Black Lives Matter movement. The ad was widely criticized for selling soft drinks by trivializing the seriousness of systemic racism and violence perpetrated against black people.

It is hard to know exactly what staff at Pepsi were thinking about the ad (which they pulled within 24 hours). One industry insider speculated that, "They had data that probably said 75 percent of millennials consider themselves activists, or whatever that data piece was, so we are going to embrace the idea of activism ... but Pepsi misfired by taking a 'very broad-stroke approach' as opposed to standing for something. It's like standing for love or happiness—that's not really a stance."[72]

In the end, the public called Pepsi out for pretending to be something it wasn't, for believing in something it clearly didn't understand. Imagine you were the social intrapreneur who urged Pepsi to lend its support toward important social movements, and the failed ad was blamed on you. You would have been seen as pushing the company to stretch toward its higher self, only to flop terribly. You'd likely face intense scrutiny and retribution from your colleagues and be ashamed for failing your company.

But should you feel shame?

The answer really depends on what it was you intended. Did you intend for the company to try to be better and mess up? No. You had good intentions. Did you know they were going to produce an ad that was terribly tone deaf? If you didn't know, can you be blamed for the company not being very good at corporate activism?

It appears that Pepsi actually learned an important lesson (i.e., authenticity is important). So in that sense, you may have brought something very important to the company. As it feels more pressure to participate in social movements, the company needs to get real about how it does that.

If, however, you were part of the advertising team that produced the ad and you thought the world would embrace the spot with open arms, well, then, you might feel some justified shame (but not toxic shame). It clearly shows that there was a gap between your actual and desired understanding of social activism.

In cases where shame is perhaps merited, the best thing to do is to admit immediately that you've made a mistake. Do not push responsibility onto others. Do whatever you can to swiftly and unambiguously to repair the damage. The sooner you take action, the better.

And even after the storm blows over, you'll still probably feel that all you want to do is to cover your face and hide in a closet. This is the time to reflect, and honor what it was you were trying to do. If you had good intentions, but you failed, it is time to think about what you can learn from this painful experience, and how you can come back better, humbled, and wiser.

League members have known more than their fair share of failure and occasional shame. The League is full of well-intentioned risk takers. One member, Julio Salazar, felt so strongly that failure is a moment for learning that he and four other friends launched an event called "Fuck Up Nights" (or FUN, for more sensitive ears). The evening involves three to four presenters sharing their failure stories for seven minutes, followed by a Q&A session and networking. The gathering has become a global movement to celebrate the resilience that comes from failing and doing so publicly.

At the time of writing, FUN has spread to 318 cities in 86 countries and nearly 200,000 participants gathering to celebrate failure. The goal of FUN is to help take the toxic shame out of failure and give participants a chance to understand what they can do differently the next time.

We hope this guide drastically reduces the chance that you'll take a starring role at the next FUN event. But if you put yourself out there and you fail, just know you're not alone. If your intentions were pure, forgive yourself. In time, your colleagues may extend the grace of forgiveness to you, but if they don't, the integrity between your intentions and actions is ultimately what counts.

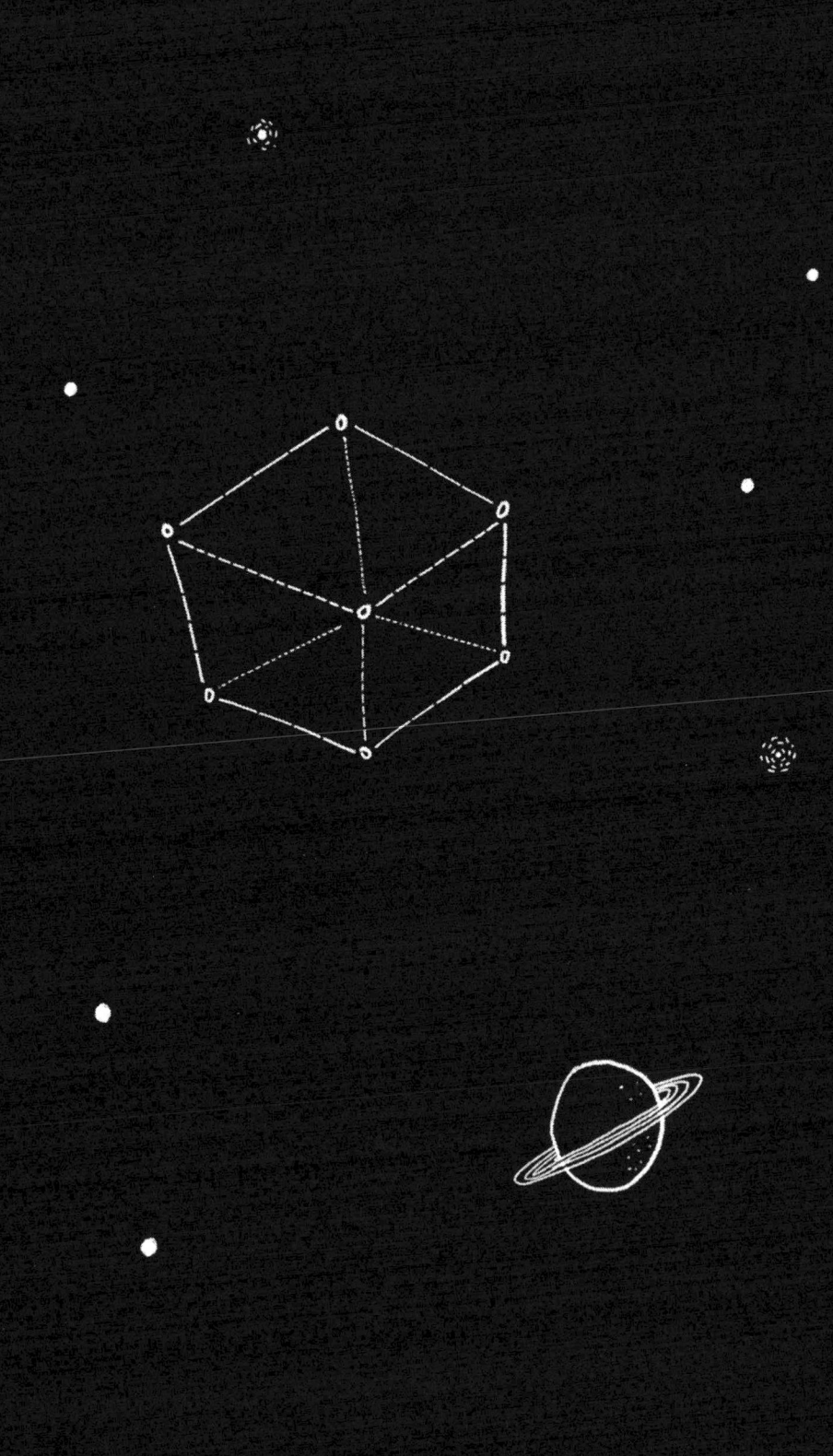

"Over the coming decades, an accelerating pace of change will test the resilience of every society, organization, and individual …
The balance of promise and peril confronting any particular organization will depend on its capacity for adaptation. Hence the most important question for any company is this: 'Are we changing as fast as the world around us?'"

GARY HAMEL, THE FUTURE OF MANAGEMENT

YOU ARE NOT ALONE!
Our League community shares some
observations from their journeys.

7

Postcards from the Field

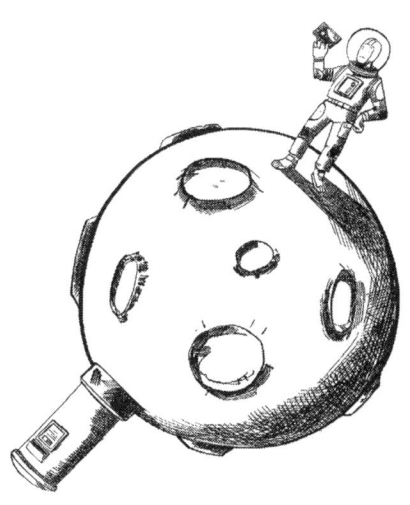

A certain Kafkaesque workplace culture has pervaded offices around the globe. The British sitcom *The Office* enjoys a viewership of hundreds of millions of people with local adaptations in nine languages.[73] The cartoon *Dilbert* runs in 57 countries and 19 languages.[74] The movie *Office Space* has become a cult classic and source of many internet memes.[75]

These white-collar comedies portray office culture as a world in which employees are dehumanized, office politics is a miasma of perverse incentives, and managers are inept, small-minded bureaucrats with racist and sexist tendencies. There are certainly great managers and great organizations, but the saying "it's funny because it's true" suggests that these comedy offerings reflect common maladaptive behavior in workplaces.

The dominant institutions of the corporate, government, and non-profit sector are facing a profound shift in societal expectations about what sort of behavior is okay in the workplace. Social media-fueled movements like #MeToo and #BlackLivesMatter make it easier for employees to demand more of their employers. Systemic pressures like climate change and global pandemics are giving rise to a new breed of employee activist and spotlighting divides and inequities across global supply chains.

Traditional institutions are feeling the operational bedrock and workplace culture rumble under their feet. The scale of change and the urgency of action demanded are obliterating the old "command and control" models of workplace management.

No longer is it strange to ask how our offices can become havens and not fodder for sitcoms about dysfunction. Or to ask why our work life can't be our life's work. Or how we might leverage our brand, innovation, people, and money to create a better world.

Intrapreneurship stands as a response to those questions. It is about employees taking charge and not turning a blind eye to unacceptable situations in the workplace. It is about finding meaning in our work and service to a cause bigger than our individual CVs.

If you're reading this book, you're probably contemplating an intrapreneurial initiative or you may already be trying to incorporate new levels of consciousness for you and your organization. Intrapreneurship as entrepreneurship on the inside represents an opportunity to harness the assets of the world's incumbent institutions to find solutions to pressing economic, social, cultural, and environmental challenges.

The web of powerful institutions across government, business, and civil society forms an invisible socio-economic and environmental system. Many, if not most, were set up for a positive purpose. Perhaps your employer has forgotten that purpose or new information has emerged that shows the original purpose is actually harmful. Your job as an intrapreneur is to help spur reflection and organizational evolution.

In carrying out your project, you and your team will experience personal growth. You may have to confront hard truths. You may have to ask colleagues to acknowledge that they have been selling a toxic or harmful product, or that the public service they have been offering disproportionately benefits the rich and powerful, or that their high-minded charity is plagued by sexual harassment and racism.

Few people happily admit these truths, and it will be your task to point out the discrepancy between the aspirational organizational identity and its actual one. The key to helping your employer push through this pain is to show that current practices are no longer working and to hold out the possibility of a future where everyone can feel proud about their organization and how they choose to spend the 90,000 working hours of their lives.[76]

This isn't a job for the faint of heart. You will, at times, feel alone in your intrapreneurial quest. When you do, we hope you'll look to the League of Intrapreneurs, a network of people just like you who believe that we can reprogram the bureaucracies of the world with fresh insight and perspective. That we can step into our office and bring our full self to work. That we can shed our skin as mere human resources and assume a more profound role as change agents for society.

We wrote this book and created tools like *The Intrapreneur's Compass* (downloadable on our website) in the hope that you will join our movement and our journey into the wild. As intrapreneurs, we cast our eyes upward with a sense that our species can do better and that we can tap our human gifts for empathy, collaboration, and creativity to solve our global challenges.

On the next clear night, gaze at the sky. You'll be joining the legions of humans who have marveled at the moon and stars, looking to the heavens to time the seasonal move to new hunting and foraging grounds. Ask yourself if it is time for you and your organization to start migrating over the next horizon.

Astronauts, extreme human explorers talk about the "overview effect" when looking down at Earth. Describing her experience in space, Anousheh Ansari, space tourist and founder of the **XPRIZE**, explains, "The actual experience exceeds all expectations and is something that's hard to put to words ... It sort of reduces things to a size that you think everything is manageable ... All these things that may seem big and impossible ... We can do this. Peace on Earth—no problem. It gives people that type of energy ... that type of power."[77]

We've now reached the end of the *Intrapreneur's Guide to Pathfinding*. As you and your fellow explorers travel through the wild terrain of intrapreneurship, may you also experience renewed faith that even the boldest, most beautiful dreams can come true, if only we dare to set forth boldly and together.

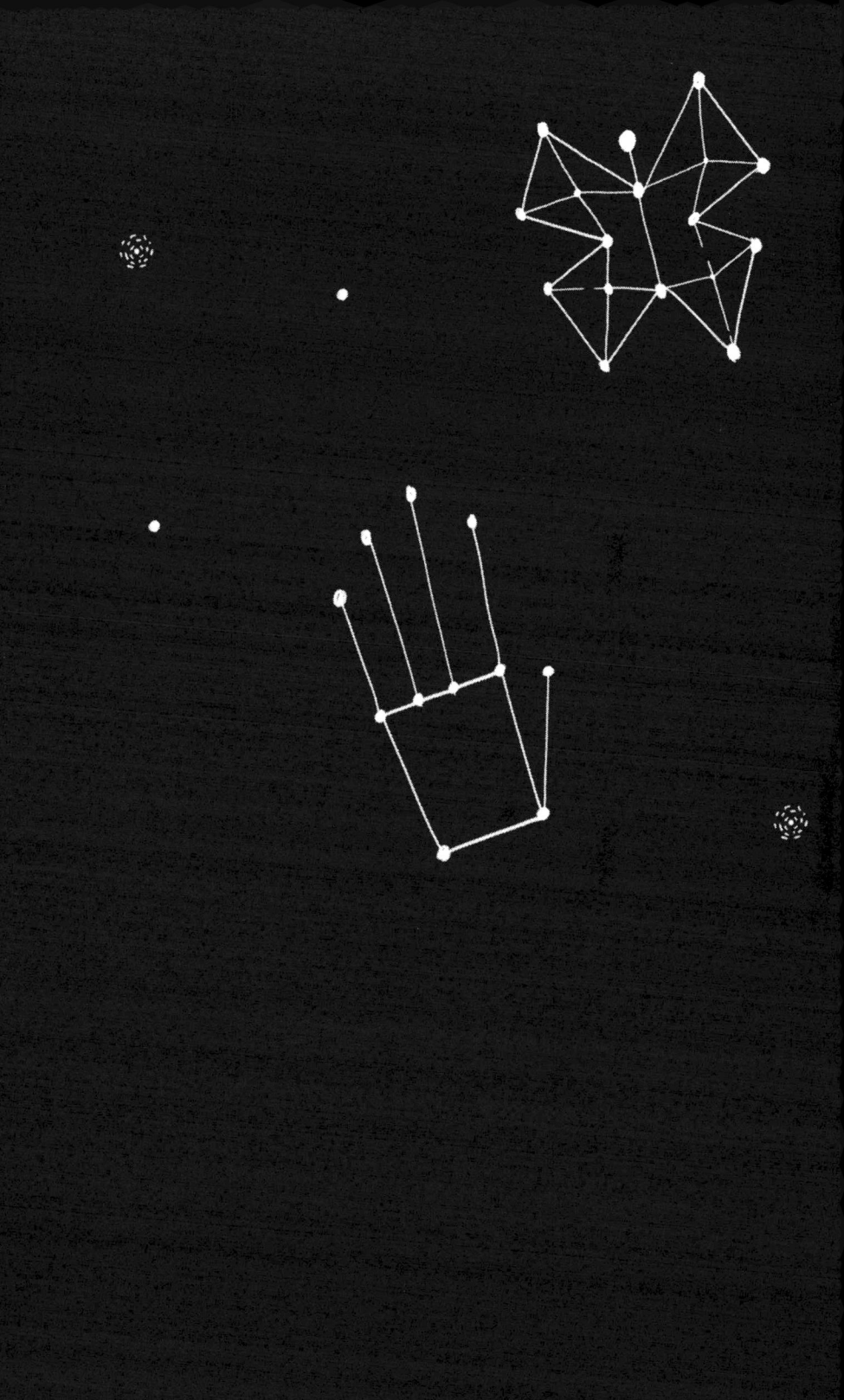

"I always tend to think about resilience in a more practical way ... it's a lot to do with discipline and commitment. You need to believe in the process you designed and the choices you made ... wake up and work: it's a mantra!"

Lucas Urbano, Intrapreneur

"We can learn a lot from athletes about resilience. In particular, the importance of dedicated rest and rejuvenation time. There isn't a competitive athlete in the world who doesn't embed rest into their weekly/monthly program. And yet for so many of us, we attempt to operate at our peak, seven days a week, 52 weeks a year. Even when it feels counterintuitive, rest time is a vital part of the process no matter what you do!"

Tessa Blencowe, League Catalyst

Think of Intrapreneurship as an Endurance Challenge!

Intrapreneurship is a marathon, not a sprint. It requires discipline and commitment. The setbacks will come, but you can stay the course by knowing when it is time to push through and when it is time to rest.

"I like to run and have learned a lot through that experience. It requires lots of discipline and commitment to continue when your whole body is asking for you to stop. The funniest thing is that once you go through that initial stress moment then you reach another state, you enter into a 'flow' and it feels you have energy again to keep on going and going."

Florencia Estrade, League Catalyst

"Focus on impact. That will maintain the fire you need to pursue your project and not give up. When you focus on impact, it is important to speak with the ones who will benefit from your project, the ones that are absolutely grateful to you for making it happen. Those people are key to sustain your force."

Lorena Muiño, League Catalyst

Find Joy in Real Impact

Keep your intrapreneurial flame alive; it will shed light on what's truly important when institutional priorities might begin to overshadow your values and goals.

"When I look back on my career, I want to be recognized for meaningful work, not that I wrote briefings very well. So my personal resilience is now stemming from a conscientious effort to worry less about the sh!t and focus more on the truly meaningful work ... Of course, dancing helps. Dancing like nobody is watching always helps!"

Ian Howatt, League Fellow

"It is my belief and experience that resilience comes from the inside of us and it boils down to whether we believe our thoughts or not. A situation happens, the interpretation we give to it creates an internal emotion ... whenever we are experiencing negative emotions we can become aware that we are holding on to an interpretation of reality that doesn't serve us. Questioning our thinking, opening the mind, transcending and opening the heart to higher emotions will lead to opening the will to take different actions and bounce back into our infinite power as infinite beings."

Rosario Londoño, League Catalyst

Embrace Emotions that Serve You;

Ditch the Ones that Don't

Taking on a powerful system will throw up all sorts of emotional turmoil for you as an intrapreneur. Some emotions can be a powerful force driving you to learn, develop, and create impact. Others will not serve you. Your challenge is to learn to let go. When we hang onto outdated practices, this is known as maladaptation and stubbornness. And in the wild, stubbornness can kill you.

THE SWAMPS OF PETTY CONCERNS

"I am always positive about my projects even though we find setbacks. Recently I had a breakdown in a project and I allowed myself to feel sad. I even dropped a few tears and got consoled by my team when I am usually the one motivating them. I have to say it felt good to embrace my feelings. For one day, I allowed myself to feel frustrated and sad. The next day I was back again, trying to learn from this setback and planning out plan B. My advice is no to hide your feelings; let them flow!"

Sofia Diaz Rivera, Intrapreneur

"Intrapreneurship is an arduous journey and most will step out at some point. It's just a matter of when. So, as you plan your initiative—consider, not only the project milestones, but people milestones as well. Who are you developing that can take things forward when you're ready to move on?"

Michel Bachmann, League Catalyst

Don't Be a Martyr for the Cause

Intrapreneurs are masters at navigating road blocks, traversing steep terrain, and shouldering stress. But, what happens when it gets to be too much? Take care not to sacrifice yourself when advancing your idea. Take stock in how much stress is enough, when to pause, and also when to abandon the quest.

"Love it, change it or leave it. Evaluating your situation regularly and taking appropriate action deliberately is absolutely important. The question, however, is when and how often you make this decision? Surely not every day. Even not every week. Maybe every three months or every year. Don't become a boiled frog: Recognize 'milestones of frustration' in order to react accordingly."

Julian Weber, Intrapreneur

"You learn a lot through failure about who are your true supporters. They are the ones still around when the project goes bust."

Shauna Alexander, Intrapreneur

Find Your People, Love Them Hard

Intrapreneurship is best undertaken in small teams. You'll naturally find champions, sponsors, and teammates who help bring your project to life.

But, what about the people who are championing YOU, the intrapreneur? Have you found your community? Are you reaching out and getting the support they are so happy to give?

"To be an intrapreneur, it is important to have a strong network around you that can help you. From the first moment, when I had an interview to become a part of the League, I started to feel that connection. Now I'm surrounded with other people that are from completely different sectors and jobs (and some similar as well!), I have found that community where we are all facing the same challenges and we are all trying to find ways to navigate through it. Sometimes we are failing, sometimes we are succeeding—knowing that everyone is doing that is a really an empowering feeling."

Katie Sims, Intrapreneur

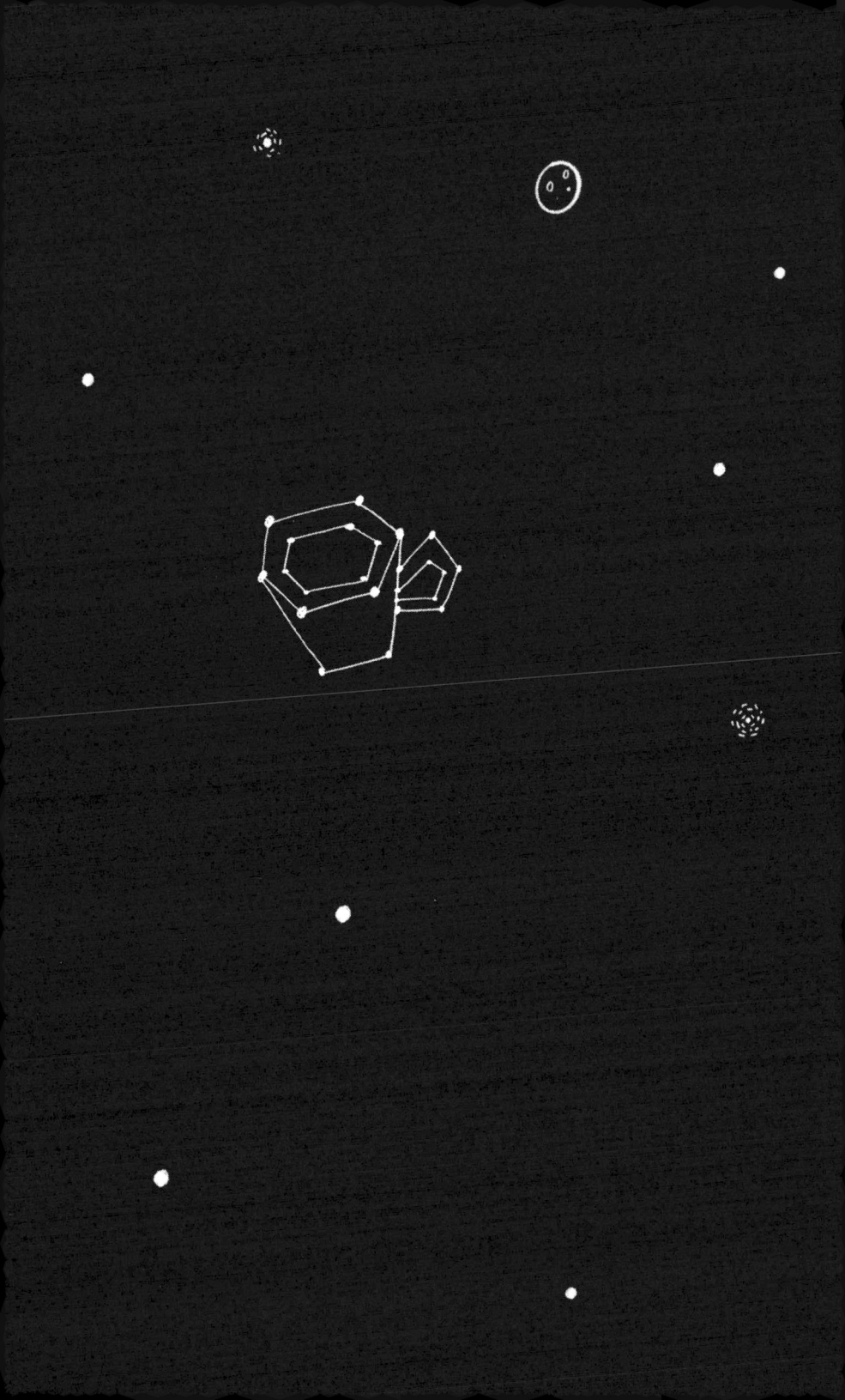

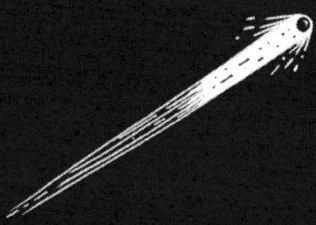

"The world doesn't change one person at a time. It changes as networks of relationships form among people who discover they share a common cause and vision of what's possible.

This is good news for those of us intent on changing the world and creating a positive future. Rather than worry about critical mass, our work is to foster critical connections."

MARGARET WHEATLEY

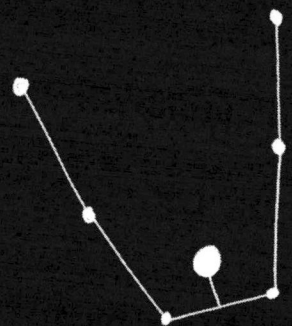

A final challenge.

We believe intrapreneurs have a pivotal role in forging a better future. We wrote this book to help fuel a movement to change our broken systems. Read it, love it, scribble on it, action it. Then think about who you could pass it onto that might just join us in changing the world?

LOVE & COURAGE,

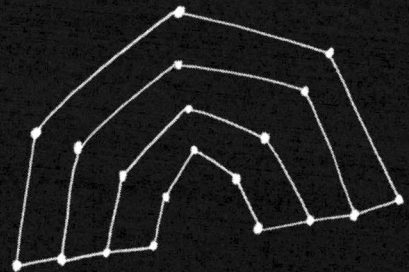

Appendix: Further Reading

Websites for Further Research

A grassroots healthcare revolution in Africa | Boris Hesser | TED Talk: https:// www.ted.com/talks/boris_hesser_a_grassroots_healthcare_revolution_in_africa

A new social connection tool helps us invest in our relationships | Swinburne University of Technology: http://www.swinburne.edu.au/news/latest-news/2019/05/a-new-social-connection-tool-helps-us-invest-in-our-relationships.php

BetterEvaluation: https://www.betterevaluation.org/

Bricolage | Wikipedia: https://en.wikipedia.org/wiki/Bricolage

Business Model Canvas | Strategyzer: https://www.strategyzer.com/canvas/business-model-canvas

Business Partnerships Fund | Business Innovation Facility: https://www.gov.uk/international-development-funding/business-innovation-facility

Change Activation: https://changeactivation.com/

Cherokee Eternal Flame: http://didahnedigakanehoi.tripod.com/Eternalflame.html

Coletivo | Coca-Cola Brasil: https://www.cocacolabrasil.com.br/institutococacolabrasil

d.school | Stanford: https://dschool.stanford.edu/

Design Kit | IDEO: https://www.designkit.org/

Don't Buy This Jacket, Black Friday and the New York Times | Patagonia: https://tcl.patagonia.com/2011/11/dont-buy-this-jacket-black-friday-and-the-new-york-times/

Final list of proposed Sustainable Development Goal indicators | Division for Sustainable Development Goals: https://sustainabledevelopment.un.org/content/documents/11803Official-List-of-Proposed-SDG-Indicators.pdf

Fuckup Nights: https://fuckupnights.com/

Headspace: https://www.headspace.com/

Here be dragons | Wikipedia: https://en.wikipedia.org/wiki/Here_be_dragons"

In Its Quest To Decrease Water Use, Levi's Is Open Sourcing Production Methods | Adele Peters | Fast Company: https://www.fastcompany.com/3057970/in-its-quest-to-decrease-water-use-levis-is-open-sourcing-production-methods

Leyla Acaroglu: https://www.leylaacaroglu.com/

Madame Mayor I have an idea | Nesta: https://www.nesta.org.uk/feature/10-people-centred-smart-city-initiatives/madame-mayor-i-have-an-idea/"

OLIO: https://olioex.com/

Resources | Presencing Institute: https://www.presencing.org/resource/tools

Saving unicorns: Making government less lonely for the trailblazers | Miki Stricker-Talbot | Apolitical: https://apolitical.co/solution_article/saving-unicorns-making-government-less-lonely-for-the-trailblazers

Shifting Diets for a Sustainable Food Future | World Resources Institute: https://www.wri.org/publication/shifting-diets"

Six Pillars of Self-Esteem: The Definitive Work on Self-Esteem by the Leading Pioneer in the Field | Nathaniel Branden: https://www.penguinrandomhouse.ca/books/17499/six-pillars-of-self-esteem-by-nathaniel-branden/9780553374391"

Susan Foley | LinkedIn: https://www.linkedin.com/in/susanfoley/

The Art of Powerful Questions: Catalyzing Insight, Innovation, and Action | Eric E. Vogt, Juanita Brown, and David Isaacs: http://umanitoba.ca/admin/human_resources/change/media/the-art-of-powerful-questions.pdf"

The Berkana Institute: https://berkana.org/

The Donella Meadows Project | Academy for Systems Change: http://donellameadows.org/"

The Essentials of Theory U: Core Principles and Applications | Otto Scharmer: http://book.ottoscharmer.com/

The League Intrapreneur Quotient™ (IQ) | The League of Intrapreneurs: https://www.leagueofintrapreneurs.com/leagueIQ/"

The Sante Fe Institute: https://www.santafe.edu/

The simple power of hand-washing | Myriam Sidibe | TED Talk: https://www.ted.com/talks/myriam_sidibe_the_simple_power_of_hand_washing"

TIME'S UP: https://timesupnow.org/

Tools for Systems Thinkers: Systems Mapping | Leyla Acaroglu: https://medium.com/disruptive-design/tools-for-systems-thinkers-systems-mapping-2db5cf30ab3a"

Ushahidi: https://www.ushahidi.com/

What is the Anthropocene? And why does it matter? | World Economic Forum: https://www.weforum.org/agenda/2016/08/what-is-the-anthropocene-and-why-does-it-matter/

Working Group on the 'Anthropocene' | Subcommission on Quaternary Stratigraphy: http://quaternary.stratigraphy.org/working-groups/anthropocene/

YourMorals.Org: https://www.yourmorals.org/

Endnotes

ENDNOTES

Introduction

[1] Allison Gramolini, "Polynesian Migration," Sea Education Association, 2011, accessed January 4, 2020, https://www.sea.edu/spice_atlas/rangiroa_atlas/polynesian_migration; Mauricio Obregón, *Beyond The Edge Of The Sea: Sailing With Jason And The Argonauts, Ulysses, The Vikings, And Other Explorers Of The Ancient World* (New York: Random House International, 2002).

[2] Joseph Stromberg, "What Is the Anthropocene and Are We in It?," *Smithsonian Magazine*, January 2013, https://www.smithsonianmag.com/science-nature/what-is-the-anthropocene-and-are-we-in-it-164801414/.

[3] "Climate Emergency Campaign," The Climate Mobilization, accessed January 26, 2020, https://www.theclimatemobilization.org/climate-emergency-campaign.

[4] "UN Report: Nature's Dangerous Decline 'Unprecedented'; Species Extinction Rates 'Accelerating' - United Nations Sustainable Development," United Nations, accessed January 4, 2020, https://www.un.org/sustainabledevelopment/blog/2019/05/nature-decline-unprecedented-report/.

[5] "Global Inequality," Inequality.org, accessed January 4, 2020, https://inequality.org/facts/global-inequality/.

[6] Brett Nelson, "The Real Definition Of Entrepreneur — And Why It Matters," *Forbes*, June 5, 2012, https://www.forbes.com/sites/brettnelson/2012/06/05/the-real-definition-of-entrepreneur-and-why-it-matters/.

[7] Elisa Alt and Thijs Geradts, "Social Intrapreneurship: Unique Challenges And Opportunities For Future Research," *Academy Of Management Proceedings* 2019 (August 2019), doi:10.5465/ambpp.2019.188.

Chapter 1

[8] "Hidden Brain: How To Build A Better Job," NPR, 2016, http://www.npr.org/templates/transcript/transcript.php?storyId=471859161.

[9] Ibid.

[10] Amy Wrzesniewski, Justin M. Berg and Jane E. Dutton, "Managing Yourself: Turn The Job You Have Into The Job You Want," *Harvard Business Review*, June 2010, https://hbr.org/2010/06/managing-yourself-turn-the-job-you-have-into-the-job-you-want; Justin M. Berg, Jane E. Dutton and Amy Wrzesniewski, "What is Job Crafting and Why Does It Matter?," Center for Positive Organizational Scholarship, *Michigan Ross School of Business*, 2007, https://positiveorgs.bus.umich.edu/wp-content/uploads/What-is-Job-Crafting-and-Why-Does-it-Matter1.pdf.

[11] C. Otto Scharmer, *The Essentials Of Theory U* (Oakland: Berrett-Koehler Publishers, Incorporated, 2018).

[12] "The Barrett Model," Barrett Values Centre, accessed January 26, 2020, https://www.valuescentre.com/barrett-model/.

[13] Diane MacKinnon, "Clean Pain vs. Dirty Pain," Diane MacKinnon, M.D., May 31, 2016, http://dianemackinnon.com/clean-pain-vs-dirty-pain/.

Chapter 2

[14] Donella H. Meadows and Diana Wright, *Thinking In Systems* (Chelsea Green Publishing, 2008).

[15] Draper L. Kauffman Jr., *Systems One: An Introduction To Systems Thinking* (St. Paul: Future Systems, Inc., 1980).

[16] Antoinette Klatzky, "What is Ecosystem Leadership?," Field of the Future Blog, *Presencing Institute*, July 6, 2019, https://medium.com/presencing-institute-blog/ecosystem-leadership-4227fd214f2.

[17] John Kania, Mark Kramer and Peter Senge, "The Water Of Systems Change" (FSG, 2018), http://efc.issuelab.org/resources/30855/30855.pdf.

[18] Natalie Moore, "In Chicago, COVID-19 Is Hitting The Black Community Hard," NPR, April 6, 2020, https://www.npr.org/2020/04/06/828303894/in-chicago-covid-19-is-hitting-the-black-community-hard.

[19] "Enduring Ideas: The three horizons of growth," McKinsey & Company, December 2009, https://www.mckinsey.com/business-functions/strategy-and-corporate-finance/our-insights/enduring-ideas-the-three-horizons-of-growth. This article was originally published by McKinsey & Company, www.mckinsey. com. Copyright (c) 2020 All rights reserved.

[20] Patrick Vlaskovits, "Henry Ford, Innovation, And That "Faster Horse" Quote," *Harvard Business Review*, August 29, 2011, https://hbr.org/2011/08/henry-ford-never-said-the-fast.

[21] Hal Gregersen, *Questions Are The Answer: A Breakthrough Approach To Your Most Vexing Problems At Work And In Life* (New York: Harper Business, 2018), 23.

[22] "The Merlin Exercise | Roadmap To Goal Achievement," Leaders Ought To Know, accessed January 8, 2020, https://www.leadersoughttoknow.com/the-merlin-exercise/.

[23] Chris Kutarna, "Mundus Novus (The New World)," *Psychology Today*, September 18, 2017, https://www.psychologytoday.com/ca/blog/age-discovery/201709/mundus-novus-the-new-world.

[24] "Natural Navigation," The Natural Navigator, accessed February 3, 2020, https://www.naturalnavigator.com/natural-navigation/.

[25] "How to Navigate with Rainbows," The Natural Navigator, October 15, 2019, https://www.naturalnavigator.com/news/2019/10/how-to-navigate-with-rainbows/.

Chapter 3

[26] Elizabeth Kolbert, "Why Facts Don't Change Our Minds," *The New Yorker,* February 20, 2017, https://www.newyorker.com/magazine/2017/02/27/why-facts-dont-change-our-minds.

[27] Martin Luther King Jr., "Letter From a Birmingham Jail," The Martin Luther King, Jr. Research and Education Institute, Stanford University, April 16, 1963, https://kinginstitute.stanford.edu/king-papers/documents/letter-birmingham-jail.

[28] "Intro to Story-Based Strategy," Center for Story-Based Strategies, accessed January 26, 2020, https://www.storybasedstrategy.org/intro-to-sbs.

[29] Ibid.

[30] Tina Seelig, "How Reframing A Problem Unlocks Innovation," *Fast Company*, April 19, 2013, https://www.fastcompany.com/1672354/how-reframing-a-problem-unlocks-innovation.

[31] Chip Heath and Dan Heath, *Made To Stick: Why Some Ideas Survive And Others Die* (New York: Random House, 2008).

[32] Tom Kelley and Jonathan Littman, *The Art Of Innovation* (Profile Books, 2016).

[33] Lorraine Boissoneault, "The Speech That Brought India to the Brink of Independence," *Smithsonian Magazine*, August 8, 2017, https://www.smithsonianmag.com/history/speech-brought-india-brink-independence-180964366/.

[34] Gifford Pinchot III, "Getting the Resources You Need: The Way of the Intrapreneurial Warrior," The Pinchot Perspective, March 29, 2013, https://www.pinchot.com/2013/03/getting-the-resources-you-need-the-way-of-the-intrapreneurial-warrior.html.

[35] "Moral Foundations Theory," moralfoundations.org, accessed January 9, 2020, https://moralfoundations.org/.

[36] David Burkus, "You're NOT The Average Of The Five People You Surround Yourself With," Mission.org, May 23, 2018, https://medium.com/the-mission/youre-not-the-average-of-the-five-people-you-surround-yourself-with-f21b817f6e69.

Chapter 4

[37] Mauricio Obregón, *Beyond The Edge Of The Sea: Sailing With Jason And The Argonauts, Ulysses, The Vikings, And Other Explorers Of The Ancient World* (New York: Random House International, 2002), 40.

[38] "AB InBev is manufacturing over 1 million bottles of hand sanitizer to donate to hospitals and frontline workers around the world," AB InBev, March 22, 2020, https://www.ab-inbev.com/news-media/news-stories/ab-inbev-is-manufacturing-over-1-million-bottles-of-hand-sanitizer-to-donate-to-hospitals-and-frontline.html.

[39] "The Basics Of Job Crafting," VMock Thinks, VMock, March 30, 2017, https://blog.vmock.com/the-basics-of-job-crafting/.

[40] Steve Blank, "McKinsey's Three Horizons Model Defined Innovation for Years. Here's Why It No Longer Applies.," *Harvard Business Review*, February 1, 2019, https://hbr.org/2019/02/mckinseys-three-horizons-model-defined-innovation-for-years-heres-why-it-no-longer-applies.

[41] Joel Gascoigne, "Idea to Paying Customers in 7 Weeks: How We Did It," Buffer, February 2, 2016, https://buffer.com/resources/idea-to-paying-customers-in-7-weeks-how-we-did-it.

[42] "Toyota and Suzuki Agree to Start Consideration toward New Collaboration," Global Suzuki, March 20, 2019, https://www.globalsuzuki.com/globalnews/2019/0320.html.

[43] "Sustainable Development Goals," United Nations, accessed January 26, 2020, https://www.un.org/sustainabledevelopment/sustainable-development-goals/.

Chapter 5

[44] Gifford Pinchot III, "Getting the Resources You Need: The Way of the Intrapreneurial Warrior," The Pinchot Perspective, March 29, 2013, https://www.pinchot.com/2013/03/getting-the-resources-you-need-the-way-of-the-intrapreneurial-warrior.html.

[45] Minna Halme, Sara Lindeman and Paula Linna, "Innovation For Inclusive Business: Intrapreneurial Bricolage In Multinational Corporations," *Journal Of Management Studies* 49, no. 4 (2012): 743-784, doi:10.1111/j.1467-6486.2012.01045.x.

[46] Gifford Pinchot III, "Getting the Resources You Need: The Way of the Intrapreneurial Warrior," The Pinchot Perspective, March 29, 2013, https://www.pinchot.com/2013/03/getting-the-resources-you-need-the-way-of-the-intrapreneurial-warrior.html.

ENDNOTES

[47] Nick Skillicorn, "The TRUE story of Post-It Notes, and how they almost failed," *Idea to Value*, April 20, 2017, https://www.ideatovalue.com/insp/nickskillicorn/2017/04/true-story-post-notes-almost-failed/; Gifford Pinchot III, "Restarting the Clock," LinkedIn, April 24, 2017, https://www.linkedin.com/pulse/restarting-clock-gifford-pinchot/.

[48] Terry Slavin, "The impact intrapraneurs: How eBay Korea broke down barriers for disabled customers," *Ethical Corporation*, October 19, 2017, http://www.ethicalcorp.com/impact-intrapraneurs-how-ebay-korea-broke-down-barriers-disabled-customers.

[49] Minna Halme, Sara Lindeman and Paula Linna, "Innovation For Inclusive Business: Intrapreneurial Bricolage In Multinational Corporations," *Journal Of Management Studie*s 49, no. 4 (2012): 743-784, doi:10.1111/j.1467-6486.2012.01045.x.

[50] "Intrapreneurship: The People'sLab4Good kicks off its second season!," BNP Paribas, May 15, 2019, https://group.bnpparibas/en/news/intrapreneurship-people-slab4good-kicks-season.

[51] Beth Jenkins, "Cultivating the Social Intrapreneur," *Stanford Social Innovation Review*, January 4, 2018, https://ssir.org/articles/entry/cultivating_the_social_intrapreneur.

[52] Vala Afshar, "FCC CIO: 5 Ways to Create Change in a Change-Averse Culture," *HuffPost*, December 6, 2017, https://www.huffpost.com/entry/fcc-cio-5-ways-to-create_b_4860704.

[53] Teresa I. Sivilli and Thaddeus W. W. Pace, "The Human Dimensions of Resilience: A Theory of Contemplative Practices and Resilience" (The Garrison Institute, 2014), 3, http://www.garrisoninstitute.org/wp-content/uploads/2016/03/The_Human_Dimensions_of_Resilience.pdf.

Chapter 6

[54] David Brooks, *The Second Mountain* (Random House, 2019).

[55] Beau Lotto, *Deviate* (Hachette Books, 2017).

[56] Robert M. Sapolsky, Behave: *The Biology Of Humans At Our Best And Worst* (Penguin Press, 2017).

[57] Gwen Lawrence, "Breathing is Believing: The Importance of Nasal Breathing," Gaiam, accessed February 17, 2020, https://www.gaiam.com/blogs/discover/breathing-is-believing-the-importance-of-of-nasal-breathing.

[58] Ed Yong, "A New Theory Linking Sleep and Creativity," *The Atlantic*, May 15, 2018, https://www.theatlantic.com/science/archive/2018/05/sleep-creativity-theory/560399/.

[59] Kelly McGonigal, *The Upside Of Stress*, 2nd ed. (Avery, 2015).

[60] Clifton B. Parker, "Embracing stress is more important than reducing stress, Stanford psychologist says," Stanford University, May 7, 2015, https://news.stanford.edu/2015/05/07/stress-embrace-mcgonigal-050715/.

[61] Daniel Goleman, *Emotional Intelligence*, 10th ed. (New York: Bantam Books, 2005).

[62] "Chai M. Tyng et al., ""The Influences Of Emotion On Learning And Memory," *Frontiers In Psychology* 8 (2017), doi:10.3389/fpsyg.2017.01454.

[63] Robert M. Sapolsky, Behave: The Biology Of Humans At Our Best And Worst (Penguin Press, 2017).

[64] Ibid.

[65] Dacher Keltner, "Why Do We Feel Awe?," *The Greater Good Science Center at the University of California, Berkeley*, May 10, 2016, https://greatergood.berkeley.edu/article/item/why_do_we_feel_awe.

[66] Michelle N. Shiota, Dacher Keltner and Amanda Mossman, "The Nature Of Awe: Elicitors, Appraisals, And Effects On Self-Concept", *Cognition & Emotion* 21, no. 5 (2007): 944-963, doi:10.1080/02699930600923668.

[67] Christopher Bergland, "Awe Engages Your Vagus Nerve and Can Combat Narcissism," *Psychology Today*, May 26, 2017, https://www.psychologytoday.com/us/blog/the-athletes-way/201705/awe-engages-your-vagus-nerve-and-can-combat-narcissism.

[68] Nainoa Thompson, "Reflections on Mau Piailug," Polynesian Voyaging Society, accessed January 9, 2020, http://archive.hokulea.com/2007voyage/2007micronesiamau.html.

[69] Navi Radjou, Jaideep Prabhu and Simone Ahuja, *Jugaad Innovation* (San Francisco: Jossey-Bass, 2012).

[70] Christian Koch, "India's ingenious approach to life," BBC Travel, September 3, 2018, http://www.bbc.com/travel/story/20180902-indias-ingenious-approach-to-life.

[71] Mikaela Cibich, Lydia Woodyatt and Michael Wenzel, "Moving Beyond "Shame Is Bad": How A Functional Emotion Can Become Problematic," *Social And Personality Psychology Compass* 10, no. 9 (2016): 471-483, doi:10.1111/spc3.12263.

[72] E.J. Schultz and Ann-Christine Diaz, "Pepsi Is Pulling Its Widely Mocked Kendall Jenner Ad," AdAge, April 5, 2017, https://adage.com/article/cmo-strategy/pepsi-pulling-widely-mocked-kendall-jenner-ad/308575.

Chapter 7

[73] "The Office," Wikipedia, accessed February 3, 2020, https://en.wikipedia.
org/wiki/The_Office.

[74] "About Scott Adams," Scott Adams Says, accessed February 3, 2020,
https://www.scottadamssays.com/about/.

[75] Billy Nilles, "Office Space Turns 20: Where Are the Stars of the Hilarious
Cult Classic Now?," E! Online, February 19, 2019, https://www.eonline.com/
ca/news/1015677/office-space-turns-20-where-are-the-stars-of-the-hilarious-
cult-classic-now.

[76] Jessica Pryce-Jones, *Happiness At Work* (Malden: Wiley-Blackwell, 2010).

[77] "Astronaut Quotes," Overview Institute, accessed January 9, 2020, https://
overviewinstitute.org/astronaut-quotes/.

Figures

[Fig. 2] *The U: One Process, Five Movements*, Presencing Institute, accessed January 29, 2020, https://www.presencing.org/aboutus/theory-u.

[Fig. 3] *Six Conditions of System Change*, FSG, accessed January 29, 2020, https://www.fsg.org/publications/water_of_systems_change.

[Fig. 4] Angus Maguire, *Illustrating Equality VS Equity*, Interaction Institute for Social Change, accessed January 29, 2020, http://interactioninstitute.org/illustrating-equality-vs-equity/.

[Fig. 6] *Moral Foundations Theory*, moralfoundations.org, accessed January 9, 2020, https://moralfoundations.org/.

[Fig. 8] *Formative to Summative Evaluation*, Meera, accessed January 29, 2020, http://meera.snre.umich.edu/evaluation-what-it-and-why-do-it.

[Fig. 9] *Sustainable Development Goals*, Division for Sustainable Development Goals, accessed January 29, 2020, https://sustainabledevelopment.un.org/sdgs.

[Fig. 10] *The Learning Zone* (adapted from Tom Senninger), Digital Academic, accessed January 29, 2020, https://digitalacademicblog.wordpress.com/tag/senningers-learning-zone-model/.

About the Authors

About Marjorie Brans

Environmental Defence Canada's Green Champion of the Year and winner of the Spirit of Lord Michael Young Award, Marjorie Brans has obsessively wondered: "Can some types of market economies be reconciled with deep care for the planet and all of its creatures?" Seeking an elusive answer, she has hunted for clues on five continents in multinational corporations, venture capital funds, tiny social businesses, and charities. To recruit and train fellow explorers for the quest, she co-founded four nonprofits that meet at the intersection of economic, social, cultural, and environmental transformation. Despite their tired feet, Marjorie and her co-travelers suspect the answer is "yes."

About Maggie De Pree

Maggie De Pree believes in the power of human agency—the ability for people to choose to make a difference in the world. She has spent over a decade harnessing the innovation potential of businesses—big and small—to address issues ranging from climate change to healthcare. Maggie is a Co-founder and Global Director of The League of Intrapreneurs and an entrepreneur and strategist, working to advance systems change with Fortune 500 companies, governments, and NGOs. She is a recipient of the Grant Thornton 100 Faces of a Vibrant Economy Award, regularly speaks and writes on the topic of sustainable innovation and intrapreneurship, and is the co-author with John Elkington of *The Social Intrapreneur: A Field Guide for Corporate Changemakers.*

About Florencia Estrade

Florencia Estrade is passionate about people finding meaning at work and how business can be an engine for positive impact in the world. She is an experienced facilitator, coaching groups throughout transformation journeys and innovation processes within different organizations and geographies. She is Global Director for the League of Intrapreneurs, after having spent more than 10 years inside large corporations including ABN AMRO Bank and McKinsey & Company, and having founded two social enterprises: an impact-based innovation consultancy and an accelerator for impact-driven startups in Brazil. She holds an MBA from UC Berkeley, is a Fulbright Scholar and Haas Merit Scholar, and certified facilitator in Theory U.

About the League

The League of Intrapreneurs is a global learning community of intrapreneurs—people working to drive systems change from within the world's most influential institutions. Members work in over 20 countries inside big companies like BMW Group, Merck, and Nestlé; inside governments like the City of Baltimore and the Australian Federal Government; and inside non-governmental organizations like WWF, CARE, and Friends of the Earth. Together, the League is working to bring #changefromwithin to create a prosperous, equitable, and sustainable world. From climate change to poverty, migration to resource scarcity, communities face systems challenges on a scale never seen before.

League members are prototyping the future of work, cultivating cultures that are more authentic, innovative, collaborative, and ultimately, more meaningful.

Visit the League of Intrapreneurs website at www.leagueofintrapreneurs.com

Printed in Poland
by Amazon Fulfillment
Poland Sp. z o.o., Wrocław

61774398R00132